17 SECRETS
OF THE MASTER PROSPECTORS

17 Secrets of the Master Prospectors

by John Kalench

First Edition / January 1994

Second Printing / August 1994

ISBN 0-9629447-2-6

Text and cover design by Jim Benson

I dedicate this book to you, Pop—
a Master of the highest order.
From where you sit, I'm sure you can see
how much I truly miss you.

Even though you are gone,
you will always be my shining light.
Everything I am and ever will be
I owe to you and Mom.

Until we embrace once again,
I remain your loving son
and best student!

CONTENTS

ACKNOWLEDGMENTS

I want to thank Master JMF (John Milton Fogg) for his creative genius and tireless contribution to this project. I also want to thank Jim Benson for his design and editing mastery.

To Jeff and Tom—my friends and past MIM associates: You've added tremendous value to both my business *and* my life. Personally, I miss our camaraderie; professionally, I acknowledge you for your courage to pursue your own path of Mastery!

Introduction

Do you really want to be a Master Prospector?

*P*rospecting is the lifeblood of your business. And, as you know, it's impossible to survive—much less, *prosper* in Network Marketing—without good, healthy blood.

When it comes to prospecting, Network Marketers the world over invariably fall into three categories:

Group One: *Those who like to prospect.* They enjoy it and are comfortable with it. They don't even think about it much. The act of prospecting flows naturally and effortlessly. This group of people are well on their way to being Master Prospectors!

Group Two: *Those who are uncomfortable with it but do it anyway.* Prospecting is *not* one of their favorite activities—to them, it's like a trip to the dentist. Yet they do it anyway, no matter how uncomfortable they feel. That's because they're highly focused on getting results in their business and they do what they need to do to make themselves successful. What's interesting is that they quickly discover that the more they prospect, the better they get at it; consequently, they begin to truly enjoy prospecting. The result: They soon graduate to group one.

Group Three: *Those who don't like prospecting at all.* Like group two, the thought of prospecting is unpleasant to them—at times, even frightening. And if their purpose and goals for doing the business are not clear and important enough to them, they choose not to do much of it. The result: Success continues to elude them.

I have no way of knowing which category you're in. I assume, though, that no matter where you find yourself, you really want to learn the secrets of the Master Prospectors and build a successful Network Marketing business. There wouldn't be any reason for you to pick up this book if that weren't true—right?

So, the purpose of this book is to help you get what you want from prospecting.

Maybe your goal is to take that first step, pushing through that initial doubt and fear of prospecting. Or maybe your goal is to polish and hone your skills to the level of the Masters themselves. Either way (or anything in between) this book will serve you!

Twice The Student

As you'll hear me say again and again... "I consider myself twice the student that I am the teacher." In addition to my own fourteen years of experience in this industry, I've been blessed to work with and learn from some of Network Marketing's "best of the best" from all over the world. I've learned how to glean all I could from what these Masters have to offer. I've learned how to match, model and mirror what they did to succeed. I've also learned how to package and present what they do in such a way that most people can easily understand it and put it to use—hopefully saving them years of trial and error, seeking and searching.

So, the purpose of this book is to share with you *proven principles* of the Master Prospectors of Network Marketing—not pie-in-the-sky theories or sheer speculation. Don't think you're going to be treated like one of those dummies in some automobile crash test! I know you're not interested in wasting your time being a part of someone else's "experiment." These secrets work! And, I promise you, if you consistently apply them, they will work for *you*.

Honesty Is My Policy

Oh, by the way, I need to clear something up with you right now. These secrets you're going to learn about aren't really *secrets*. The Master Prospectors I've worked with and studied over the years don't have any secrets. They *love* to share with others what works for them. That's one of the reasons they're revered as Masters.

Then, you ask, why do I call them secrets?

To get you to pick up this book and start reading it. By telling you this book has seventeen secrets, I got you to think—before you even picked it up—that it's special, unique and could give you something that others don't yet have.

You see, I have an unshakable faith in this book. I know it will deliver everything you expect—and much more. So I just told you what I had to (really, what you *wanted* to hear) so you could see that for yourself. And in due time, you will!

In fact, that's one of the lessons you'll learn in Secret #13: **Master Prospectors Know How To Hit Their Targets.** That secret is all about advertising and the importance of targeting your market.

Getting Comfortable

My goal throughout this book is *for you to feel more and more comfortable with this thing called prospecting*; so comfortable, in fact, that even if prospecting didn't come naturally to you before you read this book, it will by the time you're finished.

Many years ago, I had a mentor—a Master—who shared with me this very important and empowering message:

The speed at which we manifest the things we want in life is directly proportionate to the speed at which we become comfortable with those things.

Would you agree that most people are not where they want to be in life?

And it's not that people aren't capable of being where they want to be—they're just not totally comfortable with the thought and feeling yet!

As you know, our thoughts and feelings precede our actions. So if you or I aren't comfortable (in our own minds) with anything we want to be, do or have, our thinking will keep those accomplishments from us. Have you noticed how many people keep putting their dreams off somewhere into the future? That's because they're not comfortable with them *today*.

That's also why most Network Marketers are not Master Prospectors. It's not because they don't have the ability or the desire. They're just not yet comfortable with the thought or the feeling of being a Master Prospector!

So the purpose of this book is *to first help you become comfortable with that thought and feeling.*

How do you get comfortable with the thought of something? By having enough knowledge to feel secure that you can go out and try things, and by taking enough action and seeing enough results to know that what you're doing *works*.

Believe me, what you will learn in this book *works* and could change your life forever. The insights and techniques presented here have been proven in the field—where it counts—time and time again by the Master Prospectors of Network Marketing.

Competence precedes confidence, and my job here is to help you become competent at this whole business of prospecting. When you are—and it will take most of you far less time than you imagine—you will have the confidence you need to feel truly comfortable with this thing called prospecting. And you'll be well on your way to being a Master Prospector.

Get A Feel For It

Of course, there's an art to prospecting. Like any

other form of self-expression, such as music, painting or dance, prospecting is a creative field. It's much more feeling than fact. Here's the key: As you read this book, notice what feels, looks, and sounds good to you.

Why? Because the legwork has been done. I've searched, uncovered and discovered 17 Secrets of the Master Prospectors. Read them again and again. And at the conclusion of each secret, you'll have the opportunity to define the Action Steps you'll need to take to master that secret. If you really want to be a Master Prospector, then be sure to identify the steps you plan to take to do so. Your answers to the questions at the end of each secret will become your personal plan of action to becoming a Master Prospector.

So pay close attention to what feels, looks and sounds good to you as you read this book. Listen carefully to the ideas that pop into that wonderful head of yours. Make sure to write out all of the Action Steps that you believe are necessary to master each secret—and then do them! Because then you'll have the Universal "Law of Precession" on your side and that's powerful stuff. (You'll learn all about "The Law of Precession" in Secret #1.)

Oh, and another thing. Don't think that this is one of those books that you'll need to read cover-to-cover in order to understand it, enjoy it and benefit from it. (Hopefully you'll *want* to read it all the way through because you'll like it so much that you can't put it down!) Even so, I wrote this book so that all 17 Secrets would stand on their own—sort of like seventeen books within a book. Any or all of these 17 Secrets are yours for the taking, so feel free to skip around to the ones that suit you best. Just remember to apply your Action Steps to those secrets!

Don't Miss Out On Anything

Now you may find one or two of these secrets that you don't care for much—secrets that you don't feel very comfortable with, or attracted to at first. That's okay. But I'll give you an additional, bonus secret right now:

In the secrets that you're not very comfortable with, there's something special for you to discover.

Master Prospectors have learned that when they hear about something that really works—even if they don't like the idea much at first—they put aside their feelings long enough to take a deeper look. More often than not, they find a little vein of gold in there somewhere! A little something that they can dig out, shape and polish—and eventually use. So, please, make sure you don't miss out on anything these special treasures can offer you.

So, do you really want to be a Master Prospector? Are you ready to learn 17 of their secrets?

Great. Let's get busy!

Secret #1

Master Prospectors don't sit on their assets

---

*M*ost people think that the purpose of education is to gather knowledge. The real purpose of education is to *take action!*

Education is not about doing the right things. It's about learning from what we do. We can spend a long time gathering knowledge about how to do something "right," but we're not really sure how it's going to turn out until we take action. Action is where the rubber meets the road. And I don't mean just any action, although any action is better than no action. I'm talking about taking *big action*.

For example, if you want to clear the fence, you could aim for the space just above the fence. Maybe you'll make it and maybe you won't. But if you shoot for the moon, even if you fall short, you'll clear the tree tops!

That's what taking big action is all about. When you think big, your chances of getting big results are that much greater.

Mistakes?

You bet. You'll make them. Maybe even big ones! But if you're going to make mistakes—make big mistakes. You learn quicker, and—have you noticed?— you get a lot of people's attention.

Small mistakes can easily go unnoticed. Consequently, we have a tendency to repeat them. Big mistakes usually hit us right between the eyes, hard enough that we can't help but say to ourselves one of these two things:

"Wow, that didn't work. I knew it wouldn't. I shouldn't have tried it to begin with. I'll never try anything like that again." Or:

"Well, that didn't work—back to the drawing board. There's got to be a better way to do this. I mean, look at all the people out there making it work for them. I *know* I can make this work for me, too."

Big mistakes—if we're in the "growing" frame of mind—are the kind of experiences that can teach us invaluable lessons and build our character.

Master Prospectors make big mistakes because they have what I call a *bias for action*. Being in action, big action, is one of the keys to their success. That's what education is really all about: learning how to risk and take those big actions which can bring about the best of all possible results.

And if that's what you want—the best of all possible results—then you'll never be content with what you already know. You'll be a *learning machine*:

You'll take action—the bigger the better—and you'll watch what happens and learn from it. Then you'll take action again, and so on.

Making Educated Choices

The whole point of acquiring knowledge is to enable you to make more educated choices.

No matter who you are or what you're doing at any given moment in time, you always have a choice. *Life is all about making choices.* The more experienced and educated your choosing, the better your results in life. That's just common sense. By being in motion, then stopping, looking at, and listening to the results your actions generate, you constantly improve the level of the choices you make.

How do we make more educated choices? By having more experiences.

How do we experience more? By being in motion— by constantly taking action. And the bigger the action, the greater the educational experience.

I know people who've been working for twenty years. In reality, what they've actually experienced is one year, repeated twenty times. They've been doing the same old thing, over and over.

Early on in their careers, through their actions, they found something that worked for them. Some special technique, approach or strategy that when they used it, produced a favorable result. Their mistake was to think that what they did couldn't work bigger and better. They chose to ignore the possibility of a greater return for a greater investment. It's kind of like they developed this asset and then sat on it for twenty years.

Master Prospectors don't sit on their assets. Master Prospectors are never content with the status quo of what they know and do. They are constantly stretching themselves, seeking new challenges and new learning opportunities. They are constantly in motion and constantly taking action. Thus, they are able to make more educated choices.

The Shortest Distance

One reason for naming our company "Millionaires In Motion" is because we believe that the shortest distance between where we are now and where we want to be is our willingness to *be in motion.*

You may have heard the saying that the shortest distance between point A and point B is a straight line. That's true—only if you're in motion.

Personally, I've found it easier to move towards what I'm attracted to first and then adjust my direction (my line) as I go. If I waited for nothing but "straight lines" all my life, I'd never have left my mother's bosom.

Now, please, don't get me wrong. Planning your direction is vital stuff and can mean the difference between failing and succeeding. Planning without motion (action), however, always proves fatal.

So, yes, plan your actions and then act on your plan!

Just remember that your level of success will

more than likely be measured on how well you adjust your plan while you're already in motion.

To The Moon!

As an example, America's space program, NASA, launched several spaceships to the moon and successfully completed their mission to land a man on the moon and return him safely to Earth. Planning was very important on these flights—so important that the entire course was mapped out in every detail.

So, let's say that the moon is point A and the Earth is point B. Since the experts at NASA knew exactly where the moon was (they could see it), you'd think they could have drawn a "straight line" to it—thereby planning to make each journey as short and as safe as possible.

However, once the spaceships took off, would you like to make an educated guess as to what percentage of the time they were actually on course (on line) toward their target—the moon?

The experts say less than 3%. So what were they doing 97% or more of the time?

Correcting. Adjusting. Getting back on course!

We don't have the luxury (like NASA) of knowing precisely where our target is. It's not like we can clearly see it and draw this perfect "straight line" towards it before we blast off. Sure, we can hold a vision of it and estimate what it's going to take to get there. But most of the time it's still a leap of blind faith.

So what's the lesson here?

Well, your success in Network Marketing—your making $5,000, $10,000, or $50,000 per month and more—will not be based on how straight of a line you draw from where you are to where you want to be. Your success will more than likely be determined by how fast and willing you are to correct and adjust the actions you take *now!*

The Key To Becoming
A Master Prospector

So the key to Secret #1 is taking action and putting yourself into motion and then having the wisdom to correct and adjust your actions to stay on course.

And the key to becoming a Master Prospector in Network Marketing will be how well you apply the lessons you learn from this book. How quickly you identify and follow your Action Steps of Mastery for each secret. And how willing you are to correct and adjust your actions as you journey along your path.

It's during this process that you'll discover the special prospecting techniques that work best for you. When you find one, remember to keep asking yourself, "What can I do to make this work bigger and bolder? What big action can I now take to accelerate this entire experience?"

Like all Masters, don't sit on your assets—don't sit on your successes. Look to your successes as stepping stones that are paving the way to an even brighter, more fulfilling path—what many call the path of Self-Mastery!

There's a universal law I promised to share with you earlier. I believe it will help you better understand the power of motion and how it relates to your

Network Marketing business. (Just a reminder that a universal law is a law of the universe that always applies—*always!*)

The Universal Law Of Precession

Buckminster Fuller was one of the most extraordinary thinkers of all time. Our world was blessed to have experienced his wisdom and innovative ideas. He came up with a new and more accurate map of the world—the Dymaxion Map. He discovered and explained synergy and developed the Geodesic Dome. He coined the term "Spaceship Earth." Bucky, as his friends called him, was a tremendous man—a true Master in many ways!

One of his greatest contributions was what he called the Law of Precession—what I call the Law of Side Effects. Here's what it says:

When a body is in motion towards another body (because of gravity or because it's simply attracted to it), then always—at a 90° right angle to that line of attraction—there is an equal if not a greater result that's being generated.

Let me repeat that in a slightly different way:

If an object is attracted to a second object and is moving towards it, another result will occur at a right angle. That result will be equal to or greater than the original attraction.

Would you like an example?

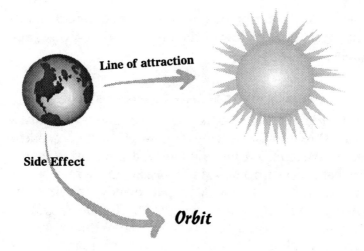

Here we have the Sun—a heavenly body in motion. Another heavenly body in motion is the Earth. You would agree that the Earth is attracted towards the Sun. Yes? In fact, there is a gravitational force there—the Earth is attracted to the Sun so much that it wants to fall towards it.

At a 90° right angle to this line of attraction, the Law of Precession creates a side effect—it's called the Earth's orbit. I'm sure we'll all agree—this is a very beneficial side effect. So beneficial that it keeps all of us from becoming toast! (Maybe here we should give thanks to the Law of Precession for saving our assets?)

Another example is a bee (a body in motion) and a flower (another body in motion).

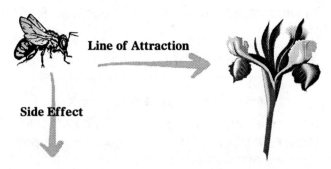

Line of Attraction

Side Effect

Cross-Pollination

Would you say that the bee is *attracted* to the flower? Right again! The bee loves to move towards the flower because the flower contains the essential nectar that bees require to make honey—the food that bees need to live.

Now at a 90° right angle to this "pull" (this attraction) is the extraordinary side effect of cross-pollination. You see, the flower's pollen sticks to the bee's body and legs. As it flies from one flower to another, the bee provides our planet the beneficial *side effect* of pollinating and fertilizing the flowers, enabling the plants to procreate their species. The end result: the plant kingdom that we enjoy so much!

To me, the most fascinating part of this Law of Precession is that the so-called "side effect"—occurring "inadvertently" at a right angle—is often the most powerful aspect of the entire attraction. I mean, where would we be without the Earth's orbit? Where would the plant kingdom be without pollination? And where would the Earth be without the plant kingdom?

Okay, so how does this Law of Precession affect

you in Network Marketing, and more specifically, what impact does it have on you becoming a Master Prospector?

Great question!

What Are You Attracted To?

Ask yourself this: Why are most people attracted to Network Marketing? Why do most people put their name on a distributor application?

To make more money?

Yes! Money is the number one reason why people get involved.

Okay, let's say this is you: a body in motion (let's hope so, anyway!) that is attracted towards another body in motion—money!

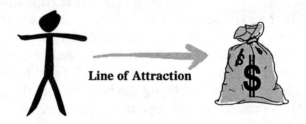

Line of Attraction

Now, I ask you: Have you ever witnessed people, regardless of their profession, who pursue money above all else? In other words, money is the only reason why they do what they do? Do you know people who focus solely on their need for, and acquisition of, money?

Think about this for a moment. What side effect does the Law of Precession frequently create for them in their lives? *Greed*?

Have you also noticed the *imbalance* they create in other areas of their lives as well—like health, family, relationships, and so on?

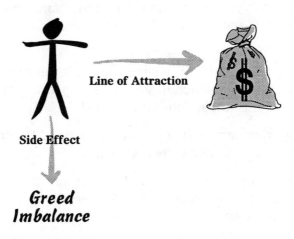

Now I'm not one who scoffs at money or thinks that it's bad. On the contrary, I've seen more good come out of the result of having money than having no money at all.

The Truth About Money

We need to be wise enough to understand what money is and what it is not. And money is nothing more than a tool, an instrument that allows us to express ourselves and function freely within our world. Alone, money is nothing. It's what we do with it that determines whether or not it has value.

I also believe that there is an abundance of money and wealth on this planet—enough for every man, woman and child on earth to be financially free. And I truly believe that everyone deserves to be prosperous and wealthy.

What's my point?

Just as the Earth's attraction towards the Sun and the bee's attraction towards the flower is natural and good, so is your attraction to money. Wanting money is healthy and positive. So move towards it—you deserve it!

My point is this: I'm sure you don't want to create greed and imbalance in your life as precessional effects of this attraction—am I right?

So what can we do to direct the Law of Precession to produce the side effect we want?

Well, my friend, we simply focus our attention on *adding value* to everyone and everything we touch along the way.

Contrary to popular belief, success doesn't lie in the *destination* of achieving a certain amount of money. Success lies in the *journey*—the day-to-day pleasure and joy of what we do in pursuit of money. When money becomes the *cause* of what we do, we can easily compromise who we are and what we want to be. When money becomes the *effect* of what we love to do, then we're being true to ourselves.

What happens next in this process is that we experience more and more *abundance* in all areas of our life—abundant relationships, an abundance of love, contribution, health and joy.... We also discover a deeper sense of inner peace, harmony and *balance*.

So you see, we don't have to deny our attraction towards money. We can use that attraction to generate richness throughout our life and the lives of everyone we touch by focusing our day-to-day attention on *adding value*.

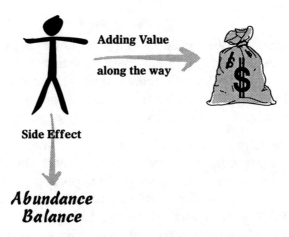

Abundance Balance

You've probably heard people state that part of their life's purpose is to make a positive difference in other people's lives. That's exactly what I'm talking about here. You can bet that these people will enjoy all the richness life has to offer—*including money*—as a powerful and profitable side effect.

That's why so many people eventually fall in love with Network Marketing. Even if their first attraction to the business was to earn large sums of money, their passion for the business grows as a natural result of *adding value* to others along the way.

Master Prospectors are well aware of the Universal Law of Precession. Their attraction towards adding value to others is just as great, if not greater, than their attraction towards money.

Their love for the *process* of their business shines through in all they do. In return, the universe and the Law of Precession rewards them with abundance, balance and money.

Feeling Like A Million

Because of this sense of purpose and balance that they experience in their lives, Master Prospectors feel comfortable with themselves. Of course, these feelings naturally move them towards an even greater perpetuation of their wealth and prosperity!

There is a joy inherent in running your Network Marketing business, and it comes from the day-to-day contribution and service you give to others. In fact, it's almost impossible to truly prosper in Network Marketing without having added a tremendous amount of value to others along the way.

Think about this for a moment. Is it possible to earn $5,000, $10,000, or $50,000 a month and more in Network Marketing without having made a positive and lasting contribution to hundreds—or thousands—of people along the way?

I don't think so!

We can't say that about a lot of industries. In fact, there are some organizations that reward people for holding back value from others—like some governments and politicians we may know.

That's one reason I hold so much faith, hope and promise for Network Marketing's future in our world. A world that is changing so quickly. A world that is moving feverishly towards global peace and away from war; towards compassion and understanding and away from prejudice; towards democracy and free enterprise and away from dictatorship and monopolies; towards honesty and cooperation and away from deceit; towards human values and adding value and away from greed; and finally, towards a method of global distribution (whose time has come) called Network Marketing and away from business practices that are rapidly proving ineffective.

So, my friend, *get off those assets!* Life offers you choices: educate yourself—study the Masters—and then boldly take big action. Think big, plan big, and stay focused on your goal. You'll make mistakes—all Masters do—so correct and adjust quickly as you move along. Master the Universal Law of Precession by adding value to everyone and everything you touch. As your sense of fulfillment, balance and purpose increases, so will your income. And in your pursuit of Self-Mastery and financial freedom, you're sure to make a direct and precessional difference in many people's lives along the way.

Great movements of change are all around us. The potential for a much greater quality of life for all is within us. Through your commitment to Network Marketing, the opportunity to blaze a path that others will eagerly want to follow is yours—and along that path, I promise you, lives your legacy!

They say that the journey of a lifetime begins with a single step. Well, your journey to become a Master Prospector begins with this secret *and* the Action Steps that follow. So complete them now!

MY ACTION STEPS

to Mastery of Secret #1

Master Prospectors
don't sit on their assets

1) As I build my successful Network Marketing
   business, how do I see myself *adding value* to
   others along the way?

_____

_____

_____

_____

_____

_____

_____

_____

_____

_____

_____

_____

_____

_____

2) Knowing I deserve to be prosperous and abun-
    dant, what side effects do I want to create in my
    life as a result of my attraction towards money?

_____

_____

_____

_____

_____

_____

_____

_____

_____

_____

_____

_____

_____

_____

_____

_____

3) What actions (the bigger the better) can I begin
    to take that will move me towards my goals?

_____

_____

_____

_____

_____

_____

_____

_____

_____

_____

_____

_____

_____

_____

_____

_____

_____

Secret #2

———

Master Prospectors
are consistently consistent

———

*E*very business—in fact, every endeavor of any kind that I know of—has its peaks and valleys. Economic trends, business cycles, seasonal changes.... People want more or less of this or that at different times. These are things over which you and I, for the most part, have no control.

But there are other highs and lows which we can and must control—that is, if we want to be a Master Prospector.

In my years of studying the Masters, I discovered that all of them have mastered one thing in both their attitude and their approach to the business: *consistency.*

They are consistent. They are consistent. They are consistent. And they are consistent—consistently.

They've learned how to minimize the emotional highs and lows that are synonymous with building a Network Marketing business.

Simply put, Master Prospectors don't allow themselves to get caught up in the roller-coaster ride of other people's emotions. Why? Because more than anything else, the emotional ups and downs of this business take the ultimate toll on most Network Marketers.

Now, another thing I've learned over the years is how powerful it is to use illustrations to make a point. So here's a graph to explain what I'm talking about. Let's take a look:

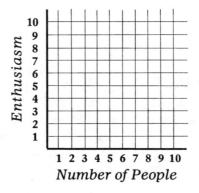

Number of People

Okay, the vertical side of the chart represents a person's level of enthusiasm, and 10 represents the most excited and the most enthusiastic one could possibly be. You may have been there yourself. Or maybe you've witnessed someone new to the business who's so excited that they're about to explode! They fly out of a meeting with their feet barely touching the ground and their tongues unable to keep up with what's going on in their head!

The bottom, horizontal line represents the number of people a person would talk or listen to in the normal course of a day, week, or month, depending on how active he or she is in building their business.

The Law Of Averages

The Law of Networking Averages says this: Out of every ten people to whom we *thoroughly* communicate the business opportunity, approximately three of them will enroll in the vision and put their name on an application. Their intention is, of course, to do something with the business. Out of those three, one of them will fulfill their commitment to some extent and go on to produce some measurable results.

I'm not saying that he or she will become the next Gold or Platinum or Executive or Emperor distributor in the company—although they may just do that. I'm saying that they will actively pursue the business.

Now here's the key to unlock the secret that separates those who are merely once-in-a-while distributors from the Masters.

Go Get 'Em, Harry!

Let's use the example of a brand new distributor who's just starting out, and let's call him Harry Hot-To-Trot. Harry has just heard the presentation and he's extremely excited. This is exactly what he's been looking for his entire life. What an opportunity—this is fantastic!

Okay, it's now one day later and Harry has just emerged from his very first Saturday training with an arm full of marketing materials and a head full of proven how-to's.

Hot? You bet.

Excited and enthusiastic? Absolutely.

So let's make Harry a 10 and put him at the top of the enthusiasm chart.

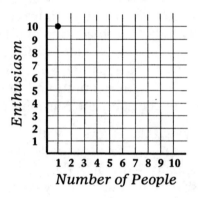

Number of People

Then Harry talks to his very first prospect, the number one name on his list—someone *certain* to say yes. And guess what?

"Nope, it's not for me. Besides, these things don't work. They're pyramid schemes, Harry. How could you be so stupid? Boy, you're going to lose all your money while some other guy gets rich and you're going to look very, very foolish."

Harry says, "Thanks, Dad."

Yes, he's a bit disappointed (and knocked down a couple of notches to an 8), but in the training session, they warned him this might happen.

So Harry says, "SW, SW, SW—*Next*. Some Will, Some Won't, So What—*Next*." (Someone in his upline must have given him a copy of my book *Being The Best You Can Be In MLM*.) As a result, Harry picks himself back up to a 9 on the enthusiasm chart and moves on to the next person on his prospect list— Mom.

Although Mom and Dad haven't agreed on anything for ages, they do on this one. Mom says, "No. And I'm not interested in the video. Get a real job, Harry, like your brother"—who happens to be the next person on Harry's list.

By the way, Harry's about a 6 on the chart now—a bit bloodied and shell-shocked.

He stops by to talk with his brother—who's just gotten off the phone with Mom and Dad—and before Harry can say "Opportu...," his brother is showing him the want ads in the local newspaper. This drops Harry's enthusiasm down to around a 3 or 4.

After calling his sponsor, who does a good job convincing him that he needs to be at tomorrow night's opportunity meeting, Harry gets pumped back up again to an 8. He also decides that talking to family members is the wrong way to go. So he heads out to talk to his buddies down at the health club.

A few more no-win conversations take place and Harry is still Hot-To-Trot, but only because that's his name. Frankly, Harry is bummed out and wonders how he ever got involved in this Network Marketing thing in the first place.

If we look at the graph and connect the dots that show Harry's fluctuating levels of enthusiasm, we see that his "line of excitement" resembles a graph that measures one of California's worst earthquakes. If he gets another "no" or two, he just might drop off the chart all together. He'll quit. Harry will be history, which is what zero on the chart stands for.

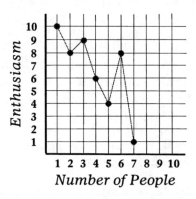

Number of People

So What Happened?

Back when Harry was a 10 and bursting with enthusiasm, there was something missing. Something fundamental and vitally important.

It's called *personal belief*, and no matter how much juice and excitement a person has, if it's not supported by a similar level of genuine *belief*, the chances of someone succeeding are slim-to-none.

Enthusiasm = Personal Belief

In the "science of attitude," there's a universal law stating that enthusiasm equals personal belief.

Why? Because belief is a lot like gravity: No matter how enthusiastic you are, your beliefs will pull on your excitement until both your enthusiasm and belief are congruent.

The reason Harry slipped so quickly is that his be-

liefs (when he started out) were so far below his enthusiasm that eventually his beliefs pulled him down
to *his* reality.

You see, even though Harry's enthusiasm was
high when he started, his belief system hovered
around a 3 or 4.

It's easy to get all excited and pumped-up by some
peak experience or moment of motivation, but if a
person doesn't really and truly *believe* in those possibilities, he or she will crash. It's inevitable. You can't
sustain an enthusiasm of eight with a belief level of
three or four. It's just not possible.

What Personal Beliefs Are Important In Network Marketing?

Here they are: a belief in yourself, a belief in others,
a belief in your company and product, and a belief in
your industry. Without these beliefs, all the enthusiasm in the world is just a house built on sand. A few
strong waves of negative emotion come along and the
house gets washed away.

That's what happened to Harry and all the Harrys
or Harrietts you may know.

When there's such a large gap between enthusiasm and belief, a person is vulnerable to being
bounced up and down by circumstances and emotions. Sooner than later, he or she is bound to get mentally and physically exhausted.

Master Prospectors walk around with an 8.5 on the
enthusiasm chart and a minimum of 8.0 on their belief chart. They maintain such a small gap between
those two numbers that they are virtually immune to
the bouncing that Harry experienced. What's more,

they're always working actively to raise their belief level. They know that just as negative beliefs can drag their enthusiasm down, positive beliefs can boost it up to greater heights than ever before.

That's why you find Master Prospectors constantly studying, learning and experiencing more—about themselves, others, their company and products, and their industry. They never stop because they know the law: enthusiasm = personal belief.

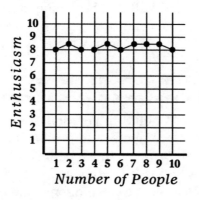

Number of People

While other people are getting bounced around, a Master Prospector, as you can see, only experiences a slight dribble—at most. He or she knows how vitally important it is to *keep* that level of enthusiasm up around 8 and 9 so they can be consistently consistent.

And *belief* is the key.

Master Prospectors work on their belief systems more than anything else. They read voraciously and listen to tapes. They attend meetings, rallies and conventions all the time. They have a huge appetite for learning all they can about themselves, others, their company and products—and their industry.

Without a firm foundation of strong personal and professional beliefs, you can be bounced like a rubber ball from emotional high to psychological low. And anything bounced enough times quickly loses air.

So consistently build your beliefs and you're well on your way to becoming a Master Prospector.

How Do I Do That?

I just love the questions you ask me!

When it comes to belief in yourself, don't let anyone steal your dreams! Strengthening your relationship with yourself is the most important thing you can do. Grow to love yourself more and more as each day passes.

Build a solid foundation of self-esteem and self-worth deep within your mind and heart. A foundation so strong that it allows you to build a bridge to the stars. As you journey through this book, you'll get some powerful tips that will help you do exactly that.

When it comes to belief in others, understand the paradox that is inherent in your business. I'll preface my explanation by asking you a question first:

Is it true that your success will be directly dependent upon the level of service you give to the people that you choose to serve?

Yes! That's absolutely true!

Well, the paradox, my friend, is this: You must refuse to think like the people that you choose to serve.

Why? Because if you think like them, you become them. And if you become them, you can't serve them—unless you're there to serve them coffee or lunch.

But if you're there to serve them—by *leading them*—to all-new heights of accomplishment and glory, then most of the time you're going to have to think the opposite of them.

And in order to do that, your personal belief system has to be so strong—so unshakable—that they cannot weaken it.

You see, some of the people coming into your network—those same people you are there to serve and lead—will occasionally try to challenge your belief system. They'll test your belief system by trying to sell you theirs. They'll try to get you to buy into their belief system when things are not going as well for them as they had hoped. They'll be coming to you with excuses—why things aren't working—instead of solutions.

And if you buy into their excuses, then you've bought into the belief system of a follower, not a leader. You've now become one of them!

Try looking at it this way: If the belief system of the people you serve had served them so well over the years, then they wouldn't be banking on your belief system to lead them in an entirely new direction, would they?

So, as a committed leader, you need to start looking for others in your network or upline who want to lead. Surround yourself with these leaders. Create a tight, inner circle of committed individuals who are willing to think and act in accord with their own strong beliefs—beliefs that may be the exact opposite of the "masses."

Meet regularly with them (maybe once a week) to brainstorm and mastermind ways to better serve the people in your network—those same people (whether they realize it or not) who are banking upon your belief system and strong leadership.

Remember this: *A great leader has a stronger belief in the potential of his people than his people have in their own potential.* So lead your people by refusing to compromise your beliefs about what's necessary to be successful. Because when it comes to building this business, chances are good that you, as their leader, know what's better for them than they do.

When it comes to belief in your company, connect with the mission of your company and make sure it's in alignment with your own.

Look beyond the company brochures and convention speeches and get to know the real people behind the principles of your company.

Every great company has great leaders with a greater cause and vision. Learn as much as you can about your company's mission and make it your own. It's a company's cause and vision that fosters integrity and sustains longevity!

When it comes to belief in your products, be your *best* customer. No one should use your products more than you. Nothing will instill higher levels of belief in your products than your own personal experiences and testimonials.

When it comes to belief in your industry, learn to love it at least as much as you love your company and your products.

Why? Because it's the industry of Network Marketing that's providing you the opportunity. Your company is like a vehicle. A vehicle you have chosen to drive you from where you are to where you want to be. Network Marketing provides you the road—the infrastructure—the opportunity—to drive and to get there!

When you truly love Network Marketing, you're in the driver's seat. You don't give up on the opportunity it offers you just because a vehicle didn't happen to work for you. You simply find another vehicle and keep on driving—and you don't stop until you get to where you want to go!

Please don't misunderstand me here. This message is *not* about you driving more than one vehicle at a time or having another one waiting in the garage in the event of a breakdown. When you choose a vehicle, be loyal to it, take care of it, treasure it and give it your best effort. It's been said—and I believe this— that we can wear only one hat at a time and serve only one Master!

My message to you is this: If a vehicle doesn't serve you after you've truly *given your best* to it, don't give up on Network Marketing! The path to *being the best you can be* still beckons you. Choose another vehicle—this time with even more experience and knowledge to draw from—and get moving again!

I promise you this: *As long as you don't give up on Network Marketing, Network Marketing won't ever give up on you!*

You've Gotta Love It!

Goethe, the great German poet of the eighteenth century once said, "What we do not understand, we cannot possess."

It amazes me how many people want to possess the *power* of Network Marketing yet they don't really *understand and love* Network Marketing. You've gotta love it—you've gotta love it—trust me, you've just gotta love it!

I love Network Marketing because I've studied it the way most people prepare for a college degree. And I believe that if you knew what I know about Network Marketing, you'd love it too. That's why I've put virtually everything I know about the history, present condition and future promise of this great industry into my second book, *The Greatest Opportunity in the History of the World.*

You may want to reference it and any other credible information you can get your hands on that will educate you about Network Marketing. I suggest you study Network Marketing like you study your products and your company.

Why? Because when you *truly understand* this business, you'll surely fall in love with it. Only then will you possess all of its glory and power.

So Once Again...

To be consistently consistent like the Master Prospectors of Network Marketing, you need to build an unshakable belief system in these four critical areas:

- Belief in yourself

- Belief in others

- Belief in your company and products

- Belief in your industry

When you do this, you'll be well on your way to becoming a Master Prospector. It's as simple and as powerful as that. Believe it!

_____

While we're on the subject of belief, I believe it's time to identify the Action Steps you plan to take to master a consistently consistent attitude and approach to your business.

MY ACTION STEPS

to Mastery of Secret #2:

Master Prospectors
are consistently consistent

1) Regarding the strengths and weaknesses of my personal belief system—where do I currently stand? (Circle the word that best describes your current state.)

A. Belief in Myself

Very strong   Strong   Average   Weak   Very weak

B. Belief in Others

Very strong   Strong   Average   Weak   Very weak

C. Belief in my Company and Products

Very strong   Strong   Average   Weak   Very weak

D. Belief in Network Marketing

Very strong   Strong   Average   Weak   Very weak

2) On a scale of one to ten—with ten being the strongest—how do I rate my current, overall belief system? (Circle one.)

10   9   8   7   6   5   4   3   2   1

3) What can I begin to do to strengthen the average or weaker areas in my belief system?

Action Steps to strengthen my belief in myself:

_____

_____

_____

_____

_____

_____

_____

Action Steps to strengthen my belief in others:

_____

_____

_____

_____

_____

_____

Action Steps to strengthen my belief in my company and products:

_____

_____

_____

_____

_____

_____

_____

_____

Action Steps to strengthen my belief in Network Marketing:

_____

_____

_____

_____

_____

_____

_____

_____

Secret #3

Master Prospectors know what their job is— and what it is not

---

*T*here is an old Chinese philosophy that says:

> *When you have been given a gift of great value,*
> *You are now obligated to return the favor many*
> *times over.*

The reason the Chinese honor this philosophy is because they believe in this Law of The Universe:

> *What goes around, comes back around.*

One surefire way to stimulate a continuous flow of valuable gifts into our lives is to share, many times over, our blessings (our gifts) with others. As the Law of The Universe states, the more good we share, the more good comes back.

Master Prospectors honor this law and embrace

the responsibility inherent in it. Master Prospectors understand—they are now *obligated* to do a job!

The job of the Master Prospector is to *share their gift*—to return the favor that has been given them— with as many people as possible. Their product and their opportunity is the valuable gift that was once shared with them. Their job now is to simply share this gift with everyone they can, in order to perpetu- ate the good that has come into their lives.

The Master Prospector's job is not to judge who's ready to receive this gift. That's the prospect's job. Master Prospectors just focus on doing their job—the sharing.

Pearl Hunting

Tom "Big Al" Schreiter tells a wonderful story about pearls and oysters that I would like to share with you. (Think of this story as a gift Tom gave me and I'm simply returning the favor.)

In every bucket of one hundred oysters, there are an average of ten oysters which contain pearls. Hunt- ing for pearls is a lot like prospecting for serious business builders in Network Marketing.

Most new distributors will pick an oyster out of the bucket, open it up, and see there's no pearl inside. Then they choose to do something very interesting. They carefully place the two halves of the oyster shell back together again, hold it tight and keep it warm. Then about every week or so, they open it up again to see if it's grown a pearl.

What's interesting is that *they know there are pearls hidden away in ten of the other oysters in their bucket.* Yet they insist on keeping that one oyster cozy and warm, hoping that one of these days they'll open it up and, *voila!*—a pearl, at last!

Well, my friend, the only way to find those ten pearls is to open up all one hundred oysters. And the chances of someone doing that are pretty slim if they spend all their time keeping empty oysters warm in the hopes that they'll magically grow pearls!

The secret in Secret #3 is *to keep shucking* (opening) *oysters!* That's your job!

A True Master

I have a friend in Network Marketing who's made a fortune. Last year he earned over $1.5 million! He certainly qualifies as a Master Prospector.

Would you like to know his secret?

He talks to twenty-five people every day. He's a pearl hunter and he just shucks oysters all day long.

When he finds an oyster without a pearl, he neatly and gently puts it back in the "ocean of future pearls" and reaches for another. He *knows* there are plenty of pearls out there. He finds ten of them in every hundred oysters he shucks.

"That," he says, "is a fact!" It's not his job to *grow* pearls. That's the oysters' job. His job is *finding* pearls. And he knows if he just keeps shucking oysters, he'll find his fair share of pearls—and more.

Drowning In A Sea Of Information

My business background before Network Marketing was in medical sales. It's a technical field and I got to be pretty good at it. When I first came into Network Marketing, I brought all of my expertise from my successful medical selling career along with me. After all, I thought, selling is selling—right?

Wrong!

With my medical buyers, I had to give powerful presentations—convincing arguments that proved that my products and services were superior to everyone else's. So when I got into Network Marketing, I did what I did best: sit down with my prospects and convince them of the tremendous value of my opportunity.

I'd give prospects an hour-and-a-half-long presentation that would just blow them away! Tons and tons of compelling information delivered with years of professional sales skills behind it. All great stuff!

If, at the end of my jam-packed, sweep-them-off-their-feet presentation, the prospect couldn't see the "wonderful" of what I was offering them—*I'd go nuts!*

I'd want to go over to them and hit them upside their head and say, "What's the matter with you? Do you have brain damage or something? Wake up! Why can't you see this?" It was like opening an oyster, finding no pearl, and then taking an hour or two to convince that oyster to grow a pearl!

Talk about brain damage. Here I was telling an empty oyster to grow a pearl!

Your Job

The Master Prospector's job is not to convince—it's to *sort.*

Master Prospectors *share* their gift. They don't try to force it on people. They don't try to convince people how valuable it is. They simply share it. They share their gift in the best and most positive way they know how.

Why? Because that's their job.

The job of the prospect is to say "Yes" or "No."

And, incidentally, either answer your prospect gives is the right answer. Why? Because in their mind it's right. In their mind it's the answer their job calls for. And it will continue to be the right answer until *they decide* to change jobs!

One Too Many Jobs

I know some Master Prospectors who come right out and tell their prospects what both of their jobs are!

After they've built rapport with their prospect, and just prior to presenting them their product and opportunity, some Master Prospectors will say something that sounds like...

"You know, Chelsea (a lovely name, isn't it?), over the next thirty minutes or so, I'm going to share with you information about the company I'm associated with—the people behind it, their vision and integrity. I'll also introduce you to the products or services we offer—what they do and why so many people are so excited about them. And then I'll quickly share with you an opportunity to earn as much money as you'd like, while having the freedom of working for yourself.

"Now, Chelsea, if by the end of this short presentation, you don't see any value in this for you, I can respect that. I realize that this is not for everyone. But at least I informed you about it so that you could decide that for yourself.

"However, if you do see value, I would like to discuss that value with you, so if you choose, I can help you get started immediately. Does that sound okay to you, Chelsea?"

Everyone understands that it's okay to do their job. No undue pressure—no hard-core convincing or manipulation. Just a simple process of informing and sharing.

So focus on doing your job—the sharing. And do it to the best of your ability. Constantly look for ways to improve the quality of your presentation (the packaging) of your gift. Then have the wisdom to give your prospect the space to do their job, too.

It's not as if your job isn't demanding enough as it is. Couple that with doing your prospect's job as well, and you begin to understand why so many new distributors break under the workload.

Some Students Teach

One last thought while we're on the subject of "what goes around, comes back around."

Recently, while conducting a seminar in Portland, Oregon, a student came up to me at the break—not with a question, but with an observation. I had been talking about the Masters of Network Marketing.

"I love studying the Masters," she said.

She had been in Network Marketing only a few months. Her enthusiasm for her newfound opportunity shone like beams of bright, colorful sunlight pouring through a large stained-glass window.

She was a member of a local association sponsored by the sales leaders and distributors in the area. They had their own center for conducting meetings and trainings.

She told me that in Portland there were less than a handful of Masters—true leaders and superachievers! Everyone else was either coming or going, and only a few were working feverishly on their path of Self-Mastery!

"Some distributors are complainers," she stated. "They seem to take every possible opportunity to talk to others about what is wrong with this or that or so and so."

She was amazed at how some distributors (usually the same group) chose to perpetuate the negative whenever any obstacle or challenging circumstance surfaced within the group.

She went on to say this:

"However, the Masters—those handful of leaders I look up to and aspire to be like—think and function quite differently. They try to fix things if they can, or rise above them if they can't. One thing is for sure: They don't wallow or live in the negative.

"Now at first I thought their reason for having a positive attitude about everything was basically self-serving. You know—they have to paint a rosy picture all the time because their bonus check depends on it. That's what the naysayers were telling me, anyway.

"Then I overheard how one of the Masters handled

a couple of distributors who were doing their complaining thing to him about something or someone.

"He listened intently to their story of discontent and blame, and then confronted them with two direct questions.

" 'Am I a part of this problem?' he asked the complaining distributors.

" 'No,' they responded.

" 'Am I a part of the solution?'

"Once again, after a brief thought, they both replied, 'No.'

" 'Then,' he said, 'I choose not to be a part of it at all!' "

BAM!

"That's great," I said. "What happened then?"

"Well," she explained, "with a courteous smile, he excused himself and walked on. The two distributors just stood there, not knowing what to say to each other. You could see their energy shift as their minds processed the experience. At first they seemed torn between personal rejection and enlightenment. By the end of the day, they were energetically working towards resolving their own problem!"

She told me that she learned something very valuable that day. As she shared it with me, I found myself becoming a student of one of my students—and loving every minute of it.

Her lesson: If the Law of the Universe called "what goes around, comes back around" is true (and from what I've seen, it *is*), then we should all be very careful what we perpetuate—what we send around.

This doesn't mean that we should go through life every minute of every day being positive, just for the sake of simply being positive. Our attitude must have meaning and purpose.

Master Prospectors appear positive and eternally optimistic because their thought process is conditioned to seek solutions.

If Master Prospectors are hit with a negative that has nothing to do with them ("not their job"), they immediately rise above it and out of it, forcing those who have the problem to begin with to deal with it!

If they're confronted with a negative situation that has something to do with them ("their job"), they act quickly in a positive way to affect and correct it.

Either way, their attitude and actions appear immediately positive to everyone around them. And what they receive in return is positive—immediately!

A wonderful lesson and a great gift. And I think she did a great job sharing it, don't you?

———————

Now, if you'd like to master the principles in this secret, here's "your job": complete the Action Step exercises on the following pages.

MY ACTION STEPS

to Mastery of Secret #3:

Master Prospectors know what their job is— and what it is not

1) Have I been doing more convincing than sorting with my prospects? (Circle one)

Yes or No

2) If "yes," what can I do or say in my presentations to help me sort more and convince less?

_____

_____

_____

_____

_____

_____

_____

_____

_____

_____

_____

_____

3) In reviewing my list of prospects and business associates, who are the oysters that I am currently trying to keep warm in the hopes that someday, they will grow a pearl? And should I continue doing so?

Name	**Continue?**	
_____	Yes	No
_____	Yes	No
_____	Yes	No
_____	Yes	No
_____	Yes	No
_____	Yes	No

4) Do I find myself listening to negative, complaining people? If so, what can I do to rise above them and effect positive changes in my life?

_____

_____

_____

_____

_____

_____

_____

_____

_____

Master Prospectors know what to marry

---

*T*his secret has a similar message to that of Secret #3. It, too, has to do with knowing what your job is and what it is not. Yet there is more, much more! Secret #4 is all about what you should marry yourself to.

In The Beginning

I learned an important lesson when we first began our company, Millionaires In Motion. At that time, we were one of the only (if not *the* only) "generic" training and development companies working exclusively within the Network Marketing industry. As we traveled around the world giving seminars, I discovered a phenomenon—which I readily admit, had me very perplexed at first.

When I speak to audiences, I just love to look into people's eyes and get as close as I possibly can to them. It's important to me to get a feel for what they're thinking. How they sit, their posture, their eyes and facial expressions are strong indicators to me.

The phenomenon I witnessed was that no matter where I was—how small or large the audience—the people attending could always be divided into three categories.

The first group were those who really enjoyed it and got tremendous value from the message I shared. Many of these people would even come up to me, and with appreciative, sincere eyes, say something that sounded like, "Thanks a million, John. You've really made a difference for me. Keep up the good work."

Now when someone acknowledges you for your contribution, it makes you feel pretty good, yes? It makes all the hard work and sacrifice up to that point worth it!

The second group were those who were still processing what they heard. They weren't quite sure what to do or what to think. They appeared a bit confused. I could even see their mental wheels turning. It's not as if they didn't like what they heard—they were merely mulling it over, trying to decide if and how it could work for them.

You see, new hopes and promises—and with this group, new doubts and fears—had just entered their mind and they were forced to deal with them. Their previous belief system had been challenged in some way, yet their mind was open enough to welcome an opportunity to view things differently.

As I watched and chatted with them, I felt all they

needed was a little time and encouragement to hear more—and to hear it more often.

The third group were those who weren't ready for what was being said at all. I could tell by the way they looked that they were reacting unfavorably to what I was saying. I can remember imagining that as they left the seminar, they would say something to someone that sounded like, "Oh, I've heard all that stuff before. It doesn't work. It's only fancy talk from a fancy talker. He's just getting rich selling everyone his books and tapes."

As you can imagine—I hated imagining that!

I Kept Asking Myself... Why?

What really got to me—and what I couldn't understand at first—was that this was the *same* seminar and the *same* presentation.

I didn't say different things to different people. This was the same message, in the same room, to the same people.

Why, I kept asking myself, did some people get it? Why did some seem confused and not quite sure what to do? And why did some people think and react negatively?

When In Doubt—Research

Like you, I take my work seriously. I'm not just up in front of a room for the applause and recognition. My work is an extension of my purpose and I want to be judged on the contribution I make to people. I chose this "job," and I want to be the best I can possibly be at it.

So, as you can imagine, when I'd experience these negative thoughts, it affected me deeply.

I know... "Don't take it personally, John." I'd tell people that all the time. Yet there I was, allowing these negative people to hurt me—to affect my attitude. What concerned me most was that maybe there was something missing in my presentation that didn't allow these people to get the message. Maybe I was doing something wrong. So I conducted a research project to see where I might be "off" and what I could do better.

As part of my research, I talked with a number of other successful speakers and trainers from a wide variety of fields and disciplines. Boy, did they open my eyes.

Each and every one of these men and women who made their living speaking and training told me they'd observed the very same phenomenon: that there were three groups of people, a small percentage of which were naysayers. These trainers told me that no matter where they went or how good their presentation, there was always that small group of mockers, complainers, and negative people that would put down what they said—or even try to put them down personally. My fellow speakers told me, "John, you have to realize that everyone is just doing what they're supposed to do."

One special friend and mentor of mine put it this way; "John," he said, "for you to think that a negative person would do anything else other than think and react negatively is pretty foolish of you—wouldn't you agree? That's exactly what they're supposed to do. It's kind of like their job."

He then added, "And these people will stay in that job—in that attitude of being negative, until they are good and ready to change. And there's nothing you or I or anybody else can do about it until then."

Well, that sure made me think. Later that night, as I lay in bed processing his words, it reminded me of Reinhold Niebuhr's famous *Serenity Prayer:*

> *God, grant me the serenity to accept*
> *the things that cannot be changed,*
> *the courage to change the things I can,*
> *and the wisdom to know the difference.*

Out Of Control

Does it make sense to you to focus your creative energies on the things that you can control, release the things that you can't, and be wise enough to tell the difference?

Of course it does. That's the essence of Secret #4: **Master Prospectors know what to marry.**

There are some people that no matter what you say or do, their job is to put you and your offer down.

Did you hear what I just said?

It's not enough for these people to say, "I don't think so—this is just not for me, but thank you for sharing it." They have got to try and put the messenger down as well.

Why? Because that's the *only* way they can feel like they're in control—while in reality, they're showing the whole world around them how out of control they truly are!

Tell me, do we have to agree with someone to recognize their enthusiasm and acknowledge their attempt to share it? Not at all!

It's one thing to say, "No, thank you." It's another to reject altogether the spirit in which it was offered. Isn't it much easier to deal with our feelings of personal disappointment when someone graciously declines our offer?

I'm sure we're all wise enough to know that no matter how "good of a thing" it is we have to share, it's not going to be for everyone!

It Takes Courage

Whether your prospect accepts or embraces your way of thinking is not as important as their willingness to hear it to begin with.

You see, it takes *courage* to listen to other people's ideas and to be open to change.

Why courage? Because without courage, everything remains the same. Nothing is ever challenged and nothing is ever changed. And tell me, where is the truth—or the good—in that?

It's not as if everything is as good as it's going to get. Change is inevitable. Change for the better is paramount. And it takes courage for someone to even entertain the thought of change!

It's Not About You

You simply must not take a negative person's words and actions personally—as difficult as that sometimes seems.

Why? Because it's not about you. You're simply

the messenger. It's the *message* that they're not ready for. And if it appears as if they're reacting negatively to you, the messenger, it's probably because they lack the courage necessary to entertain the thought of change in the first place.

I'm going to repeat that to make sure it soaks in:

It's not your fault if someone reacts to your message—your gift—with negativity. It's probably because they lack the courage necessary to entertain the thought of change in the first place.

Your daily challenge is to be wise enough to see that.

Why? Because that's the only way you'll maintain the stamina necessary to consistently and enthusiastically share your message with others. And it's those countless others out there—those millions of others who are willing and waiting to hear your message—that are depending on your stamina.

So Say "I Do!"

Two things you can control are: the *quality* and the *frequency* of your message. So marry yourself to them.

Marry yourself to the *quality* of your message—have a mad, passionate love affair with it! Make a commitment to your message. Nurture it, treasure it and be loyal to it.

Take every possible opportunity to improve your relationship with it. Occasionally use audio or videotape to review yourself sharing your message with others. Listen and look for ways to improve the delivery of your message.

Count the number of questions you ask your prospect. Look for ways to ask more questions that will get your prospect more involved. Listen for "danger words" that you may be using out of habit, like "sign-up," "buy," "cost," "sell," and so on. Replace them with more empowering words such as "join," "invest," "retail," and the like. Make your presentation better and better—make it the best it can be!

Marry yourself to the *frequency* of your message as well. Commit to sharing your gift with someone every day! And don't go to bed that night unless you've done so. All of this you can and must do.

Can? Yes, can. Because you can control all of that.

Must? Yes, must. If you truly want to *be a Master Prospector.*

Well, are you ready to marry and master your message? Great! Say "I do," and begin your Action Steps *now*.

MY ACTION STEPS

to Mastery of Secret #4:

Master Prospectors know what to marry

Knowing that I completely control the *quality* and *frequency* of my message...

1) What are some of the things I can do to continually improve the quality of my presentation?

_____

_____

_____

_____

_____

_____

_____

2) How many times each week do I commit to present my products and/or opportunity to others?
   (Circle your choice)

   1 to 3   4 to 6   7 to 10   11+

3) What will I need to do to put these appointments
   into motion each week?

_____

_____

_____

_____

_____

_____

_____

_____

_____

_____

Secret #5

———

Master Prospectors have a magical genie

———

As I work with thousands of people all over the world, it's surprising how many new distributors believe that they are going to build a highly successful network based on the circle of influence (the people) that they already know: their family, friends and associates. Unfortunately, for most of them, that's not going to be the case.

Let's say that while walking on the beach one day, you find a magic lamp. One of those old, ornate brass lamps that looks so real—like Aladdin's magic lamp—and you just know there's got to be a genie inside. You rub the lamp, and sure enough—*Kazaamm!*—a cloud of swirling smoke appears and out pops this huge, towering, magical genie.

Now, the genie's there to grant you a wish, right?

So the first thing the genie does is bow low to the ground and say, "Master, your wish is my command."

So far so good—yes?

As you think for a moment, you glance over at the genie. He has this look on his face that says, "Come on, Master, what about it? There are millions of people who'd give anything to be in your position right now. What's your wish?"

So, you say, "Genie, my wish is for you to zap me three years into the future. I want you to show me the enormous network I will have built. Show me the thousands of prosperous, happy, financially free people who will have come into my business and are living the life they always dreamed of. Being able to see this, genie, would be great inspiration for me."

So the genie waves his magic wand and—*Ali Kazap, Ali Kazaam!*—there you are, looking down on this vast network of excited, enthusiastic Network Marketers. You see thousands of successful business builders. People laughing, sharing, having the time of their lives. Among them are hundreds of your top leaders: training, inspiring people, and building enormous networks of their own.

You glance back over at the genie and he says, "Very nice, Master. You're right, this is quite inspiring."

Surprise, Surprise!

As you hover over this large, highly successful network enterprise of yours, you can't help but notice something very interesting:

There's not one face there that you recognize!

So you turn to the genie and say, "Genie, I don't see anyone I know. I don't recognize a soul. These people, these friends of mine—they're all strangers!"

The genie lets out this booming laugh, making the earth rattle and shake. He then leans down to you and says, "That's true, Master. *That's the magic of Network Marketing.*"

And magic it truly is.

Why? Because chances are that the best business builders in your network three to five years from now are people you haven't met yet! You have little or no idea who they are or where they're going to come from.

This leads us to one of the most powerful tools that you can put to work for yourself immediately as a Master Prospector: the power of creating instant rapport and making positive first impressions with everyone you meet.

You Only Have One Chance...

"You only have one chance to make a positive first impression." We've all heard this many times before, and for good reason. And when you realize that you have yet to meet your future superstars, the power of the first impression becomes even more important.

Master Prospectors know that it's hard to tell who's going to turn out to be a future leader or business builder. Many high-powered professional people such as doctors, lawyers, engineers and real estate agents have come into our industry like a house on fire only to drop out within the first few months.

Conversely, some of the most unlikely folks you'd

ever meet have risen to the top of the Network Marketing ladder: maids, bartenders, sixty year-old housewives ("I haven't worked in over thirty years!"), raw college kids, down-and-out folks from all kinds of business backgrounds.... They've become superachievers.

The point?

Remember when every American believed that anybody could grow up to be President? In Network Marketing, anybody—and I do mean *anybody*—can reach the uppermost positions of success and accomplishment—financially, organizationally, personally, professionally—you name it!

So since that first impression you make on your prospects could be the impression that starts them along their great Network Marketing highway of possibilities, it needs to be the best impression you can possibly make. Wouldn't you agree?

I Already Know You!

The people we know already have an impression of us. This is especially true of our family, friends and close associates. Like it or not, they usually have put us in a box marked this or that.

It's natural. The people who've known us for a long time tend to think of us as they always have. I know that when I met some of my high-school friends at our thirty-year reunion, they couldn't believe that I'd become who I've become. They still thought of me as I was back then: quiet, shy, sometimes even nerd-like! It's hard to change the impressions people hold onto from the past.

But with new people—with people you've just met for the first time—you've got a clean slate. You have the opportunity to create any impression you want—anything!

If you're highly positive and professional, their impression of you and your product will be highly positive and professional. If you're negative or doubting, that's the impression they'll be left with.

That's why it's so important to understand the power of the first impression.

How do you do it? How do you make the best possible first impression?

Master Prospectors Are Masters At Creating Rapport

Rapport is a relationship between two or more people where each person present is open, comfortable, relaxed and at ease. Would you agree that a person who feels that way about you is likely to listen and be open to what it is you have to say? Sure they would.

Have you ever met someone—at a social or business function—and within a few short minutes you felt as if you'd known them all your life? The conversation flowed along freely and openly, and both of you were able to share easily and effortlessly. You had so much in common—many of the same likes and dislikes, passions and pleasures. You were so interested in each other, too. It's magic when that happens, isn't it?

Now, did you know that you can actually create that kind of relationship with just about everyone you meet?

It's true. You can, when you master the art—and science—of building rapport.

Of course, there are people whose job is to avoid relationship. When you encounter someone like that, don't bother to push that rock up a hill. Wish them well and move on.

I'm sure you've encountered people who were in Grump City when you were in a great mood, up and flying high. They greeted your enthusiastic, "Hi, how are you?" with a grunt of dissatisfaction or complete avoidance. So what do you do then?

I'll tell you what *not* to do. Don't rush and gush around them trying to change their state of being. It's like the pearls we spoke about in Secret #3. There are ten pearls in every hundred oysters. When you open up an oyster that has an attitude problem—no pearl, just a bad attitude about being opened in the first place—gently close it back up and return it to where it came from.

When you encounter someone with an unfriendly attitude, move on.

You see, the vast majority of people in the world are more than willing to have a great time with you. You can go a long, long way in creating open and friendly rapport with most people—even strangers you've just met—through the use of matching and mirroring techniques.

I don't want to go into a detailed explanation here. There are excellent books written on the art and science—and it is a *science*—of building rapport. For now, here are a few tips from the latest work being done by the people who study and practice NLP

(Neuro-Linguistic Programming). NLP is the art and science of communication.

Match and Mirror

Have you ever observed people, especially couples, seated together in a restaurant? I love to do this. It's great fun. Restaurants are perfect places for people-watching.

I watched a couple just the other day, at lunch. The man talked once in a while; the woman tried to make a point, but after each sentence she looked down or away. He studied the menu and the ceiling. She fussed with her makeup, sifting through her purse. He turned away in his chair. She crossed her legs in the other direction.

I see things like this and wonder: Did they come in together or did they just come from court? Some people seem like they don't belong together at all—like they're total strangers or even enemies!

On the other hand, there are some couples engaged in animated conversation. They're laughing and making gestures with their hands. He reaches over to touch her arm. She's smiling at him and then makes a humorous face, tilting her head this way and that. Then he does the same. They seem to sit forward on their chairs, trying to get as close as possible to each other. These folks are hitting it off—they're in rapport. It's obvious to everyone that they're having a great time together.

Power Lunches

I also love to watch what's obviously a "power lunch" between business people and try to imagine what position each person holds. It's fun to try to figure out who's who. Who's the salesperson? Who's the decision maker? Who's the junior executive along for the ride? After doing this for years now, I can tell how any relationship is going by observing how the people at the table look and respond to each other.

A table where each person sits with a different posture, speaks at a different pace and looks in different directions is a group of people who are not in harmony with each other—a group of people who are *indifferent*. If it's a business meeting, you can bet that group is going to leave with the same challenges they came with.

You can also tell when people are really getting along with each other: there's a lot of mirroring going on. Mirroring is the technique of *reflecting back* a behavior or gesture of the person you're speaking to. Master Prospectors mirror someone by simply observing the things they do and matching their own behavior with that of their prospect's.

Let's look at some individual aspects of the mirroring process and use some examples:

Posture

Notice how the person you're with is standing or sitting. How are their arms positioned? What are their hand gestures? Watch how they tilt their head. Are their legs crossed or uncrossed? Are they sitting back in the chair or up on the edge of it? Standing close or far away?

Then just match or mirror that posture.

Begin to notice the different postures people have

and what attitudes those postures accompany. For example, what do you think is going on if the person you're speaking with has his or her arms crossed tightly across their chest? How about if they're sitting stretched back with their hands behind their head? What about a person sitting way back in their chair? How about sitting up front, on the edge of their seat?

Each posture is as much of a communication as the words a person is saying. In some cases, it's a more honest communication than the words. You may have heard it said that eighty percent of communication is nonverbal. It's true.

What do you make of a person sitting way back in their chair, legs crossed, facing off to the left, with his or her arms folded tightly across their chest? And what if they then say, "I'm very interested in your opportunity."

Yeah, right.

What they're actually doing is sending out a whole bunch of nonverbal signals indicating that they're not interested at all. Seems to me that, at best, they feel like they're "doing their duty" by listening to you.

So what can matching and mirroring do to make that person feel more at ease with you and open up to you more?

Try matching your basic posture with theirs. Use your body to *reflect* their body's position back to them. (That's why they call it mirroring.) After a few minutes, slowly begin to open up, turn slightly towards them, and move forward on your chair. It's called "meeting them halfway."

By the way, don't be afraid that they'll notice and think you're acting strange. They don't and they won't. It's a very subtle action on your part, yet it gets astonishing results.

If you're at a party, notice how people are standing together. Some people get really close, kind of "in your face." Others stand apart, a kind of "safe distance" away. Here's another place to mirror and match the person you're speaking with. You can imagine how disconcerting it would be for someone who likes to stand back a bit to have the other person chin-to-chin with them. Some people call this "giving people their space."

Posture is only one of the areas where you can match and mirror people. Here are some others:

Breathing

We all breathe differently. Some of us take long deep breaths. Others breathe in a shallow, more rapid fashion.

Like posture, breathing patterns also communicate. Have you noticed how you breathe differently when you're excited and happy? Your breathing tends to get faster—though it remains deep in your chest. When you're anxious, your breathing is also quick—yet it's higher up, more shallow.

You can actually match your breathing to that of your prospect's, which will result in the both of you being in breathing harmony.

Physical healers, such as massage therapists, have long realized the importance of breathing in unison with their clients. It puts them in tune. Once they are, they have the opportunity to gently shift the way the other person breathes, simply by altering their own.

So you can begin to create rapport with someone simply by matching the pattern of your own breathing to theirs.

Eye Movements

Have you ever noticed how some people look directly at you while others are looking all around, rarely "catching your eye?"

As you watch a person's eyes, match the direction they're looking in. Nothing threatens a person—who can't easily meet your eyes—more than you staring straight into theirs. Nothing displeases a person— who looks directly at you—more than you looking away, never meeting his or her glance. Matching eye movements is powerful.

Noticing a person's eyes can tell a whole story in itself. Let me tell you about one of my experiences.

Windows Of The Soul

Once we had a party at my house. It was potluck with people bringing their favorite dishes to share. I remember the wife of a friend brought a lovely Mexican dish and presented it to me at the door of the kitchen. I thanked her, took the dish and began to place it on the table with the others. All of a sudden, I noticed her eyes crinkle up. They kind of winced, almost as if in pain. I hadn't finished putting the dish down, so I stopped and said aloud, "Boy, this looks too good to just stick here. Margaret, would you move some of those other things over for me so I can put this right in the center of the table?"

If you could have seen the new look that came over her face and the sparkle in her eyes, you would never doubt for a moment the power of someone's expression. Old age wisdom says, "The eyes are the windows of the soul." In Margaret's case, they clearly conveyed her gratitude to me—and her pride in her cooking!

Here's more about the eyes: their direction. As you talk to someone, especially after asking them a question, notice if their eyes look up, side-to-side, or down. Their direction lets you know if the person is visual (eyes move up as if imagining pictures), auditory (eyes move back and forth from side to side as if attempting to hear better) or kinesthetic (eyes look down, helping them get in touch with their feelings).

Speaking Styles

Most people will fall into one of these three categories: visual, auditory or kinesthetic.

Visual people say, "I see." They speak (and breathe) more rapidly than average. They also describe things as pictures, because that's how they store their memories, and vision is the dominant sense they "process" with.

Visual people will constantly tell you how something *looks* to them. They usually have a gift for detail and describe scenes or scenarios with ease.

I've often noticed that you can have great success with visual people by speaking about "drawing a picture" for them, or "putting them in the picture."

Auditory types say, "I hear you." And they mean that, literally. Their memories and perceptions are primarily formed by sounds, voices and conversations.

Auditory people have a great respect and appreciation for the spoken word. They speak at a moderate pace and tend to be articulate and quite precise in their use of language. They are usually good conversationalists. Jokes, stories, and detailed descriptions go a long way with them.

Obviously, auditory people are excellent listeners. And, as you can imagine, they highly value your listening to them.

Kinesthetic people process with other senses, especially their feelings. These are emotional folks. They often have a tough time putting their feelings into words, but when they do speak out, their voices are soft and their speech is slow. They breathe deeply.

They're the kind of people who shake hands with *both* hands. They are huggers and touchers.

Kinesthetic people are intuitive people. Facts are far less important to them than "feeling right" about something or someone. You can bring them out on a subject by asking, "Carl, how do you feel about that?" Or, "How does that feel to you?"

Beware of dumping lots of information on kinesthetic people. You'll get a lot farther with them by *feeling* with them. Share your feelings and encourage them to share theirs.

The Master Communicators

Master Prospectors are master communicators. I'm not talking about their ability to use a bunch of techniques to manipulate people. I'm speaking about their ability to create a context for a deep and authentic relationship of communication with others.

As you prospect for your Networking opportunity, it's crucial to learn the other person's deepest concerns, desires and dreams. Most people don't walk up to strangers they've just met and talk about those things. That kind of conversation is reserved for friends, people they trust and have genuine rapport with. Yet Master Prospectors can have strangers tell them their heart's desire in just a matter of minutes.

Why? Because they've mastered the art of communication—and that starts with building rapport.

Have you ever met someone—when you were really excited about something—and you couldn't help but explode with enthusiasm? I've done that.

There I am, jumping up and down, talking a mile a minute about this and that, and anybody observing the two of us would notice the other person shrinking back, looking down, getting quieter and quieter.

It's as if I'm on the tenth floor of this skyscraper (because I'm in this high visual state), yelling down to this person on the first floor (who is kinesthetic by nature), trying to get them to see what I'm saying. Believe me, that just doesn't work.

You've got to recognize what floor your prospect is on first, and then take the elevator up or down to their floor so you can communicate on the same level. That's what this rapport building process is all about: being responsible for recognizing your prospect's level (or floor) and then going there to communicate with them.

Do you see what I mean?

Hear what I'm saying?

Feel what I'm sharing?

Great! Once you get into rapport—once you begin to communicate on that person's level and establish trust between you—you can take them up or down to whatever floor you want, to whatever floor works best for you! First, though, you've got to establish rapport so they'll want to go with you.

I Think... I Feel...

I've observed another phenomenon that works well for the Masters. Most people are usually either intellectual or emotional. (I'm sure this has something to do with right-brain, left-brain orientation.) I've discovered that when I talk to people, they either say "I think" this or that, or they say "I feel" such and so.

If you've ever heard me speak at a workshop or seminar, you'll notice I try to use both "think" and "feel" throughout my presentation. I try to include everyone in the audience so I can connect and communicate with all types of people.

I was amazed at the results when I first learned this and began to say "think" with the thinkers and "feel" with the feelers. The percentage of people who enrolled in what I was offering dramatically changed for the better!

Master Prospectors are master communicators because they are experts at matching and mirroring others. It's a key reason why they get so many more "yeses" than "nos"!

So, I strongly encourage you to study this thing called building rapport. Apply the principles you've learned here. Practice and observe how people respond and react, and as time goes on, you'll master many of these communication skills. You won't even have to think about what you're doing. You'll just meet someone and immediately begin putting them at ease. You'll quickly establish trust and have open, honest conversations with almost everyone you meet. You'll soon become what the NLP experts refer to as, "unconsciously competent."

A final note: The science of NLP is very complex and broad in scope. You don't have to embrace all of it to learn and master the rapport building process. Try it a little at a time. Remember that building rapport is a way to get into a deeper, more meaningful relationship with someone.

The world can be a pretty lonely place. As more people become master communicators, skilled at building rapport, we, as people, will grow closer and closer.

Remember your magical genie and the vision (the wish) he granted you? Your best business builders of the future will come from people you haven't met yet.

Every stranger you're about to meet is a potential Manager, Director, Supervisor, Diamond, or even Emperor! So study the act of friendshipping and building rapport, and the world, my friends, will become your oyster!

Okay, I'll bet you can *see* how you can use this secret to empower yourself. You must admit that the idea of mastering the art of friendshipping *sounds* wonderful! Are you ready to get a *feel* for what it's going to take to get there? Satisfy all of your senses and complete the Action Steps below!

MY ACTION STEPS

to Mastery of Secret #5:

Master Prospectors have a magical genie

1) When I meet people, what impressions do I want to leave them with? How do I want them to think of me?

_____

_____

_____

_____

_____

_____

_____

_____

_____

_____

_____

_____

2) What can I do to learn more about the art and science of building rapport with people? What books, tapes, teachers or classes can I study or attend?

_____

_____

_____

_____

_____

_____

_____

_____

_____

_____

_____

_____

_____

_____

_____

_____

_____

Secret #6

Master Prospectors love to build bridges

---

*W*ith the help of a "magical genie," you've seen the future, and you know that your best business builders will come from people you haven't met yet. You're now more aware of the power of making positive first impressions with people by building rapport, and you understand the Networking Law of Averages (ten pearls in every hundred oysters). So now let's take a look at the business and the art of meeting people and making friends.

Master Prospectors love the idea and the limitless possibilities of making the world their oyster. They also understand that one never knows where pearls are going to surface. They could pop up anywhere.

You could meet a pearl at a museum, a party, a restaurant, a bar or lounge, sitting in a hotel lobby, standing in a supermarket checkout line, on a train, on a plane, at a basketball game. Name a place, no matter how remote or unusual it may seem, and there's always the possibility of finding a pearl—*if you're looking!*

I know a Master Prospector who hired a maid to clean his condo. Now she's a leader in his network earning a strong six-figure income. Another Master Prospector discovered a pearl working as a bellboy in the hotel where he gave his opportunity meetings. Yet another—and this one amazes me—was in an auto accident. No one was hurt, and the Master Prospector enrolled the woman whose fender he crunched!

Want to do something fun? Ask every Master Prospector you meet how he or she met the person who got them into the business. Many of their stories will amaze you.

What's A Stranger Anyway?

Most people feel more comfortable talking to people that they already know. You know, talking to "friends" instead of "strangers."

Here's a powerful truth that the Masters live by: *A "stranger" is simply a friend you haven't met yet.*

So, if you want to be a huge success in Network Marketing—a Master Prospector of the highest order (and highest income)—make yourself into a people-meeting and friend-making machine. How do you do that?

Every Master Prospector I have ever met has a creed. It's almost as if it's tattooed on the inside of their forehead so they can always see it as they look out into the world, as they meet new people and make new friends. Here it is:

People don't care how much I know,
until they know how much I care.

That creed was first taught to me by Cavat Roberts, the founder of the National Speakers Association. If Mr. Roberts had one talent that rose above all the others he possessed, it was his ability to make friends out of complete strangers.

And making friends—or "friendshipping" as some people now call it—is a Master Prospector's stock-and-trade. So, *make a friend first!*

Too often, men and women new to our business are so anxious to get people into their network that the first thing they do when they're introduced to someone is to blurt out, "Hi, my name is Anxious Archie. Wanna become a distributor?"

Wrong!

Make a friend *first!* The time you invest in doing so will work wonders.

In Search Of. . .

Here's something else that's important to remember: When you've mastered the art of making friends, *you never need to search for prospects!*

I want you to really think about what I'm about to ask you.

Which would you rather do:

1. Recruit people into your Network Marketing business? Or:

2. Make a lot of friends?

Which has less pressure? Which requires less selling and convincing? Which is more fun to do? And which will return to you greater rewards and abundance?

The Master Prospector's answer to all of these questions is number two, "Make a lot of friends." It's the first *bridge* they build when meeting people. That's why we say that Master Prospectors love to build bridges. And the approach ramp they use to build this bridge is the first impression and rapport building skills we shared in Secret #5.

The Friendshipping Bridge

Once you've made a good first impression with someone and you've established rapport, the next step is what Master Prospectors call "friendship building."

Ask yourself this: What one thing is true about all your friends?

You may come up with a list of things, and one of the things on your list probably sounds something like this: "My friends are very interested in *me*." Yes?

A universal quality of humans is that they tend to be interested in people who are interested in them. Is that true for you? It sure is for me and all my friends.

I've shared with you before that successful Network Marketers place a high value on meeting people and making new friends. This requires a genuine curiosity in people. One quality all Master Prospectors share is an insatiable curiosity about the people they meet.

What if you don't have such curiosity? You develop it. How?

Studying Human Nature

A friend told me a wonderful story with a powerful point that I'd like to pass on to you.

Once, a noted psychologist decided to conduct an experiment to prove a pet theory he had.

He purchased a first-class plane ticket from New York to Los Angeles. The experiment was this: Once onboard the plane, he would strike up a conversation with the person seated next to him. The rule he gave himself for the five-hour flight was *that he would not say a single thing about himself.* He would only ask questions of the person sitting next to him.

He took his seat next to a gentleman, and, without introducing himself, began a conversation.

The psychologist had also assembled a team of researchers in Los Angeles who met the plane when it arrived. They whisked away the psychologist's flying companion for a quick interview.

The researchers summarized their findings with two remarkable facts:

1. The passenger told the researchers that the man sitting next to him (the psychologist who only asked him questions) was absolutely the most interesting person he had ever met in his entire life! And,

2. He did not know his name!

Interesting, isn't it?

Displaying a sincere curiosity by asking questions is one of our most powerful friendshipping tools.

The Question Is...

Which questions should you ask?

It's simple: questions that help you learn all about the person to whom you're speaking. For example:

Where do you live? (Most people are proud of where they live. If not, they've got a lot to say about that, too.) What's it like there? What do you like most about it? What's your home like? The land it's on? Neighbors? Stores? Schools? Parks and places to visit? Where did you live before? What was that like?

What about your family? Your work? What do you do for fun? Where have you traveled? The list goes on and on.

Asking questions, though, is only half of the equation. The other half is *truly listening to the answers*.

I'm Way Ahead Of You

Did you know that the average human mind can assimilate, interpret and process information 300 times faster than someone can speak that same information? No wonder our attention often wanders during conversation. We have a natural tendency to move ahead of the people we're listening to—*way ahead!*

Master Prospectors have learned how to discipline themselves to pay particular attention to what other people are saying. They're well aware of how rapidly their mind works and they know when to put the brakes on and simply *listen*.

Believe me, I know this takes effort and practice. Yet it must be done—it's vitally important to being a good listener.

You cannot listen to another person when you're busy listening to yourself. And as all Master Prospectors know, successful prospecting is eighty to ninety percent listening.

Look, it's natural to think. Hopefully, we do it often! And when we're in a conversation with another person, that person is bound to say a number of things we'd like to think about. That's the sign of a curious, interested friend. The challenge is that we cannot do this thinking and also maintain the attentive level of listening that's required for successful prospecting.

Trust—It Will Come!

Master Prospectors are not concerned with what they are going to say next. They trust that things will flow when they truly listen.

Most beginning distributors are trying so hard to think of the right thing to say—they want so much to have this person get into their business—that they're not able to listen to anyone else but themselves. My friends, it's *listening to your prospect* that makes all the good things happen.

The secret to saying the right things at the right time is listening. With your attention focused on what your prospect is saying, ninety-nine times out of a hundred, you'll know exactly the right thing to say! Just trust!

Listening is a big key to becoming a Master Prospector. Remember when I said that Master Prospectors are master communicators? Well, what do you think is more important in mastering communication: being a master talker—or a master listener?

Mine Is Bigger

Another thing to be aware of when talking (or, rather, *listening*) to a prospect is falling into the "better-than" trap. You know, when the person you're talking to says one thing and you "one-up" them. Let's say they're talking about a fish they caught once, and you top them with, "Well, you should have seen the one *I* caught up at Lake Whoppafishie..." This isn't a contest or a competition. This is about finding out all you can about this person's life and work: likes, dislikes, loves, values, experiences, dreams—*everything*.

This process can take whatever time you are willing to give it. Don't think that you have to rush it.

How do you know when the friendshipping is complete enough for you to move on?

You will notice a change in the person—what the NLP experts describe as a "shift of state." The person will assume a distinctly different posture, or he or she will laugh. Maybe their tone of voice will change and become more relaxed. Their posture will open up; they'll "lighten-up and brighten-up." Don't worry. You'll see it clearly.

Now I'm not saying that friendshipping is something that has an end. I'm just saying that there comes a point where once you've created a friend, you can now, if you choose, move on.

Move on to what? Prospecting.

And you do that by building a bridge—like the ones built by the Master Prospectors of Network Marketing. It's called a *transitional bridge*.

Getting To The Other Side

Now that your prospect is comfortable and at ease and you know a great deal about his or her quality of life, work, dreams and goals, you can now shift the conversation over to you.

How? Build them a bridge—a transitional bridge—so they can get to the other side!

This transitional bridge spans from them to you. Its goal is to move the central focus of the conversation from your prospect over to you.

Why? To see if that person is interested in looking at what you do and what you have to offer.

This is a key point. The objective is simply to get your prospect to *take a look*: an open-minded, friend-to-friend look. And that's a lot!

Master Prospectors use transitional phrases to create this bridge—a bridge that helps their prospect comfortably move from one side of the conversation to the other.

"Maybe You Can Help Me..."

One of the most powerful words in any language is the word "help." The next time you're in a crowded public place, such as a movie theater or supermarket, cry out the word "Help!" and watch what happens.

Get the picture?

The word *help* rings lots of bells. So, as a transitional phrase, you could ask, "Maybe you can help me..." followed by any number of specific approaches, such as:

"Maybe you can help me. I have a business here in town, and it's growing so rapidly that I'm looking for people interested in supplementing their income on a part-time basis with an income of between $500 to $1500 a month...." Or:

"Maybe you can help me. Do you know anyone who's looking for a career change from a workaday job to an exciting business that's got a wide-open future? It doesn't require any significant capital and the learning curve is the shortest and easiest to master I've ever seen...." Or:

"Maybe you can help me. I'm looking for people who want to earn money, but don't want to go to an office from nine to five every day. You know, people who want to spend more time at home with their kids and...." Or:

"Maybe you can help me. Do you know of anyone who is overweight and would love to quickly and easily get rid of ten or twenty excess pounds...?" Or:

"Maybe you can help me. Do you have any women friends who'd like to look ten years younger...?" Or:

"Maybe you can help me. Do you know anyone who's good with people and wants more creative control of their work, their time and their life?"

Get the idea?

Now, how do you come up with those "Do you know..." transitional phrases?

You create them based on what you discovered in your friendshipping conversation.

Those questions you asked that person about their home, family, work, and so on, have another importance. In addition to making them feel comfortable with you as a friend, they provide you with that individual's unfulfilled desires, expectations, frustrations, dreams and hopes for the future. This information can tell you whether or not this person is a prospect.

Also notice that in the "Maybe you can help me..." approach, you're not asking if the person you're talking to is interested. You're asking if he or she *knows* anybody. This "third party" approach takes the heat off them and allows them to:

1. Think of a number of possible referrals. And:

2. Personally look at your offer from a comfortable distance without getting defensive.

Master Prospectors are well aware of the advantages of a third party approach. They use it often!

Ask For "How Would You..." Advice

People love to give advice. How about you?

Now I'm not talking about gossipy, nosy or negative kind of advice. I'm talking about the times when someone regards another as an authority and genuinely seeks to know more from them. That's the kind of advice we all love to offer.

Master Prospectors seek that kind of advice all the time—*especially* from their prospects.

Here's how this transitional bridge is built:

You're there with your prospect, and, based on your friendshipping conversation, you've discovered your prospect has a unique area of expertise. Now believe me, *everybody* has one. It may be selling real estate, raising kids, playing sports—whatever. Focus on that area.

Here's an example: Let's say you're talking to a high school teacher who loves to teach:

"Bob, I'm curious. How would you go about introducing high school teachers like yourself to an opportunity that would enable them to put their powerful teaching skills to work and turn their long summer vacations into major, part-time profit centers?"

You've learned from *listening* to Bob that he takes a summer job, but it's not financially or creatively fulfilling to him.

Here's another example, this time with a housewife:

"Sarah, what advice could you give me about how I can approach mothers and homemakers to let them know about an opportunity where they could be with their families, yet earn a significant income running their own home-based, part-time business?"

By asking people how they would go about doing something, you diffuse any defensiveness. Why? Because you're eliciting their help and support. That's something people are willing to offer their friends—even brand new ones!

This approach also lets you talk more about your business, your product and your opportunity. At the risk of sounding callous or insensitive (because I'm not), it's a bit like fishing, where you cast out your bait to see if the fish are biting. And like fishing, *your job* is to cast your line in the right place at the right time. It's *their job* to take it or not.

Help Vent The Pain (The Negative)

Many times, when you've established trust through friendshipping, people will take you into their confidence and begin revealing to you what's really bugging or frustrating them in their lives. We call this "creative complaining," and it can be a valuable transitional tool.

Why? Because Master Prospectors know how to help people vent their pain.

Imagine that the pain someone is sharing with you is like boiling water in a tightly covered pot that desperately needs to vent steam. Your job is to lift the cover as many times as you need to in order to support your prospect in "getting it all out in the open." There are a number of reasons for doing this:

1. It will deepen your friendship.

2. It will allow your prospect to rid themselves of the negative, emotional charge that's *behind* their pain.

3. It will give you additional information about your prospect's needs, wants, values and desires.

The way you accomplish this is to take their side, literally *champion* their complaint or frustration and help express it fully. Use encouraging statements and questions such as, "Tell me more about that..." and, "What's that like for you...?" and, "How do you feel about that...?"

Once they've gotten it all out of their system—and you'll know when this happens when they sit back, possibly laugh, or visibly *change their state*—it's now time for what many Master Prospectors consider the most powerful transitional bridge of all.

"If I Could Show You A Way..."

Now here's where some real creativity comes into your conversation.

Take stock of all that your prospect has told you about him or herself. What are their hot buttons, their complaints and unfulfilled needs, and their richest dreams and desires? What things are most important in your prospect's life? What would make his or her life work exactly the way they've always wanted?

Once you have those in mind, match them up with the words, "If I could show you a way...."

Here's an example:

"Margaret, if I could show you a way, that, over the next six months to a year, you could start the business you've always wanted, work from your home the days and hours you choose, earn that additional $1200 a month to build that dream house you talked about and still have more time to spend with your kids than you do now—would you be willing to take a serious look at something that could provide that for you?"

Here's another: "Jim, if I could show you a way where your terrific talents with people could be put to better use, and in a couple of years, you could be earning twice what you're earning today—without having that terrible boss telling you what to do—would that be of interest to you?"

Remember, the Master Prospector's goal at this point is *not* to ask them to sign up. The goal is to have them commit to taking a serious look. And that's a lot!

Can you see how powerful this is?

After you've created a friend, listened to their complaints and helped them express their frustrations fully, can you see how someone would be willing to take a close look at a possible solution? And if they aren't, then you're probably talking to someone that enjoys living in their pain! So maybe it's time to move on.

You know, there are some Master Prospectors who find twenty-five pearls in every hundred oysters—not just ten. They do so by making friends first and building these powerful, transitional bridges to their opportunity.

About Burning Bridges

This one is short and sweet—*don't!*

No matter how bad your rapport building or friendshipping may have turned out with someone, and no matter what indifferent or negative response you may have gotten when you tried to build a bridge for someone, *don't burn the bridge behind you.*

If the person doesn't want to be friends, that's fine. Just back off. If the person isn't willing to take a look, that's fine too. Just back away. Make sure, though, to leave the bridge intact so they can return some other day.

If you don't receive a positive response or if the person puts you off, don't pout, shout or cry. It could be just a matter of timing.

Maybe it's just not the right time in that person's life for your gift. Two weeks, two months, two years or even twenty years from now could be perfect! You have no way of knowing that until you extend the bridge to them again.

Don't Slam The Door

There are many ways to leave the door open with people. One of the best is to simply ask them.

"Chuck, I can see that you're not interested right now. Would you like me to at least stay in touch with you? Maybe check back with you (or mail you product announcements, send you my newsletter, etc.) in a month or so to see if things may have changed?"

There's little or no threat in this. Most people, especially since they are aware they've just disappointed you, will say "yes" to keeping in touch.

Here's another:

"Betty, I can see you're not interested in taking a look at this opportunity now and I can understand why. Could we at least keep networking with each other? Tell me, what can I do to help you with what you're involved with now?"

Imagine someone saying, "No. I don't want your help and support. Buzz off." Hasn't happened to me yet. And I doubt it will happen to you either.

So don't burn your bridges. Keep in touch with your prospects. People's circumstances often change. As your success increases and you share it with them by simply staying in touch, sometimes that's all the encouragement they need to take a serious, second look!

When you've learned how to build strong bridges and never burn them behind you, there is always the possibility that someday, someone will want to use that bridge to come over to your side!

Like A Fine Wine...

I know many Master Prospectors who have been cultivating friendships *for years* with people to whom they wanted to offer their business opportunity. It's not that they're shy and they're stalling until they get good at their presentation. It's just that special people and special circumstances sometimes call for special considerations!

In my discussions with hundreds of highly successful people in Network Marketing, I've noticed that most of them have a number of exceptional producers in their network that have taken a long time to get into the business—several months, or even a year or more!

And you know what I've noticed about a large percentage of these people who took their sweet time to enroll in the concept? They're often the best people in that Master Prospector's network! Compare that situation to those individuals who jumped into the business the very first time they heard about it, then jumped right out again.

Like a fine wine, some prospects are just better *aged*.

Now I'm not saying that the only good people that enter your network are those who take a long time to cultivate. And I'm also not saying that the people who are excited and enthusiastic and want to start immediately will quit just as quickly. It's true that both of these do and will happen, but my point is this: Leave room in your prospecting plan for seed planting, nurturing, growing, and finally harvesting. Some things (usually the best things) can take the longest time to grow. This is true, for sure, in Network Marketing.

You may find that your prospecting efforts with some people simply amounts to keeping the opportunity in front of them long enough for it to be the right time. Be willing to invest the time that both of you need. For your efforts and persistence, those long-term prospects may some day become your pride and joy!

Don't ever give up. Remember: One of the key differences between the Master Prospectors and all the rest is that Master Prospectors stick around long enough to get paid! So stick with it.

And stick with this secret long enough to complete the Action Steps below. The following exercises will help you become a Master builder of bridges and friends, and that's powerful stuff!

MY ACTION STEPS

to Mastery of Secret #6:

Master Prospectors love to build bridges

1) What are some questions I can ask my prospects to encourage them to open up to me? (Refer to page 88 for ideas.)

_____

_____

_____

_____

_____

_____

_____

_____

_____

_____

_____

_____

2) What can I do to become a better listener?

_____

_____

_____

_____

_____

_____

_____

_____

_____

_____

_____

_____

_____

3) Of the transitional bridges used by the Master Prospectors (starting on page 91),

A) What bridges do I see myself using immediately?

_____

_____

_____

_____

_____

_____

_____

_____

B) What phrases or bridges can I create (based on my unique gift) that will move my prospects towards me and my opportunity?

_____

_____

_____

_____

_____

_____

_____

_____

_____

4) What are some ways for me to stay in touch with
    those prospects of mine who need more time?

_____

_____

_____

_____

_____

_____

_____

_____

_____

_____

_____

Secret #7

Master Prospectors use more than a pick and shovel

---

*M*aybe it's time to polish up that old pick and shovel of yours.

Just like the prospectors who panned and dug for gold back in the old days, today's modern Master Prospectors use tools to prospect for their gold. Let me illustrate this with a story.

Let's say that I, John Kalench, own a gold mine. And not just any run-of-the-mill gold mine either. I have one of the richest gold mines in the world.

Now, because you and I have become such good friends, I'm going to share my treasure with you.

You, my friend, can have all the gold you want. I truly don't care how much you take, because my mine is full of gold—lots and lots of gold.

I've only got one condition: You can only go into my gold mine once, and come out once. That's all. You have only one opportunity to prospect for all the gold you want. Fair enough?

So tell me, *what tools will you bring with you to my gold mine?*

Will you bring only your basic pick and shovel?

What will you use to carry away your gold—a saddle bag, a bucket, a horse and cart?

Would you show up at my gold mine with old, beat-up, worn-out tools?

Would you only bring a hand-held bucket to carry your gold away in?

Of course not. If you're the kind of person I think you are—the kind of person who would be reading a book about the success secrets of the Master Prospectors—I expect you'd show up with a tractor trailer or three: a team of helpers, bulldozers, dynamite and more. And that's the whole point of this secret.

You know, this story is a lot like prospecting in Network Marketing. Many times we only have one chance, just one fleeting opportunity with a prospect—the opportunity to uncover a fortune!

That's why Master Prospectors *always* have the right tools for the job. And these tools are sharp, polished, and ready to go to work at a moment's notice.

The first of these prospecting tools is:

Business Cards

One fundamental aspect of the unique concept of Network Marketing is that the Networking company takes the dollars that—if they were involved in conventional marketing—would normally be spent on advertising and promotion and invests them directly in compensating the independent distributor network.

In case you were a bit confused about their reason for doing this, let me clarify: Your company is not spending its marketing dollars on you just because they love you (although I'm *sure* they do). *They pass the savings on to you because you are performing the marketing function for them.* Instead of investing in marketing the product through radio or TV ads, in magazines, or on expensive floor displays, your Network Marketing company invests this money in what they think is a better way—they give it to you. In exchange, you become their "living ad."

Remember this: If you're involved with Network Marketing, you're paid to advertise—and if you don't advertise, you don't get paid! I think it was Mark Twain who said, "The spider builds its web in the doorway of a merchant who does not advertise."

Now if you begin to think of yourself as a walking/talking advertisement, does that open up some new possibilities on how to approach your business? Master Prospectors have mastered this, and they do everything they can to make their personal advertising campaigns as cost-efficient and results-getting as possible.

One of the simplest and least expensive methods is *business cards.*

Now a very common mistake made by many beginning distributors is to only order business cards directly from their company. Please don't misunderstand me—this is a valuable service your company offers. Because they buy these cards in such large volume for so many people, you can get your own cards quickly and at a great price. And that's a real benefit.

But what the Herman and Hillary Hope-It-Happens of Network Marketing often do is place an order for only 250 business cards from their company, and then immediately sit down to figure out how they can get these cards to last their entire networking career!

Once Again—You're Paid To Advertise

You're in business for yourself. You own your own Network Marketing business twenty-four hours a day. You're the boss, and I'm sure you'd like to attract other men and women who want to be their own boss and have their own business, too.

I'm sure you've read the news stories and possibly experienced this firsthand: There is no security in the American workplace anymore. Remember IBM and their concept of lifetime employment? These days, it's simply not a reality. Many other parts of the free world are experiencing the same thing.

And Because Of This. . .

Professional men and women everywhere are more open today to alternative employment (by that, I mean *self*-employment) than ever before. They see the changes that are taking place. They're looking for a better way.

Doesn't it make sense to capture the attention of these people? To attract them to the lowest-risk, highest-reward possibility in the entire world of free enterprise? Sure it does.

So maybe you need a business card that positions you as a *business owner*—so you can attract people that would like that for themselves as well.

Maybe it's important for you—and them—to have your own, unique business card that shows you as the president, founder or CEO of your own company.

Making It *Your Business*

Before I say more about cards, let me make a very important point:

The biggest challenge I see with Network Marketers is that most of them are not passionate enough about their business. If you're not already, *you've got to get serious about your business.*

It continues to amaze me how many people in Network Marketing still run their business through their personal or household checking accounts. How can you track the income and expenses of your business if it's all mixed up with groceries, movie money and clothes for the kids? You can't. And do you know what message this sends to you and to all the people you do business with? You're saying, "This is my hobby, it's not really a business at all."

Please, get serious about your business! Make it official.

Find a company name. File a DBA (Doing Business As) or fictitious name. Set yourself up to look, sound and feel like you're in business. Anyone that's truly serious about their business must first *have* a business!

In most parts of the world, this is not an expensive proposition at all. Check it out. Usually your local county clerk office can help you.

Bank On It!

You can use your business name to open a business checking and savings account at your favorite bank.

Then when you walk in, the bank officers can rush up to you bowing and scraping: "How *are* you, Ms. Natalie Networker? Ah, bringing *more money* in today, I see? Business must be good, yes? Can we offer you a loan? How about a new car? A new house? Oh, please, don't wait in *that* line—come over here to the special booth reserved for our business owners. How can we serve you today, Ms. Networker?"

"Thank you, Mr. Bank President," you say. "But I'm just here to deposit money into my account. By the way, you should make time to have lunch with me and take a look at a unique opportunity I think could benefit you. Shall we say Tuesday at noon—or is Thursday better for you?"

Anyway, banks *do* treat their commercial customers differently. And as a Master Prospector, your bank will treat you—if they don't already—in such a special way.

My Company Is...

Put the name of your business on your cards, checks, and stationery. How do you choose your business name? Good question.

There are two schools of thought about business names. Let's look quickly at each and you can choose the one that's best for you.

Business Name Number One: your own name. The big plus here is that many people trust a business when it has a person's name on it. People see you as a person who stands behind his or her business. Prospects will get a kind of money-where-your-mouth-is impression when the business is in your name. Examples of this are John Kalench and Associates, The John Kalench Company, etc.

Business Name Number Two: a name that tells people what you do, or what your business is about.

A young man in one of my seminars was floundering in his business building efforts. He came up to me after one of my presentations and we talked. I introduced him to the idea of positioning and the importance of choosing a dynamic name for his business. We had a good chat, and as it usually happens, I had to leave and catch a plane to my next engagement. A number of months passed, and when I saw him again, I was amazed. He looked totally transformed!

I mentioned how great he looked and asked him what he'd been doing. He pulled out his business card and showed it to me. There, across the top, it said, "The Health and Wealth Company." I looked back at him and he said, "John, I'm in the health and wealth business. Which one would you like to hear about first?"

Wow, powerful stuff!

Now, either of these two ways work—whether you use your own name for your company or create a unique one. The choice is yours. No matter which you choose, make it official. Do your business a favor— set it up to look, sound and feel like a business.

Back To Business Cards

Now I want to be clear about something: When I recommend that you get your own business cards, I am not saying that you ignore, avoid, or soft-peddle your affiliation with your Network Marketing company. Quite the opposite!

There are some Network Marketing companies today that are investing considerable amounts of money to create public awareness and acceptance of their name. Of course you'll want to take full advantage of that. My point is this:

Of the thousands of products and programs out there, you chose your Networking company! That's a choice to be proud of. Your relationship with your Network Marketing company is a very important one—they are your partners in profit.

You, however, are *your own* Network Marketing company. People don't see your corporate headquarters or shake hands with your company's CEO first. They see *you*. You are your company's CEO, and the CEO of the Network Marketing company you're affiliated with is your equal—your partner in business success.

I'm saying that *this is your business and you will be offering others the opportunity to engage in their own business as well.* Producing your own business card with your own unique identity and marketing position is a powerful step in that direction.

The Best Business Cards

Of all the cards I've tried, this is the one people remember and talk about most: business cards with your picture on them. And I suggest that the picture be in living color!

How many business cards have you been given over the years? Lots, I'll bet. How many have you kept? A lot less, I'll bet. Which ones did you hold onto? I know what I've done.

I can remember sorting through my business card collection one day, just cleaning them out. I was discarding (no pun intended) those that I thought I'd never need or use.

I came across this card with a man's picture on it. I thought to myself, "I don't know this guy. I don't need this card...." And as I reached over to toss it into the circular file, I stopped. I couldn't throw it away.

Why? Because it was like throwing *him* away! There he was in my hand, looking up at me as if to say, "Hey, John, you're not *really* going to get rid of me, are you?"

It was quite funny and I laughed out loud, but it taught me a great lesson.

I not only ordered cards with my picture, I also ordered postcard-sized photos of the entire team at Millionaires In Motion—with names alongside the faces. I can't count the number of times clients and people from our seminars have called to comment positively on those cards. People love to put a face to a name. They love to see who they're talking to. And there's a valuable marketing lesson hidden away here that I don't want you to miss.

Whom do we do business with the most? People we know—right? That's because we're familiar with them. We know them and they know us. Dealing with familiar people is naturally more comfortable than working with strangers.

Well, sticking your picture on your business card is a perfect way to increase your familiarity with everyone you meet. Including a card in all your correspondence or product orders keeps you in front of people in the best possible way.

Just A Note...

Here's a twist on the photo idea that I learned from Bob Burg. Bob's a Master Networker and the author of a dynamite tape series called, "How to Create an Endless Stream of Referrals." Here's his idea:

How many of you have a scratch pad on your desk or by your phone? We all use them. I have one right now on my desk from the automobile-detailing company that takes care of my car. Do you think I'll consider using anyone else? Do you think I think about having work done to my car when I look over to write a note to myself? Do you see how powerful it might be to have a bunch of memo pads printed up with your company name and your picture?

Bob Burg sends out a memo pad every time he mails something to someone. They only cost him a few dimes to make and mail, yet it keeps his name and business familiar with the people he wants to stay in touch with. I think it's incredible!

Every time I send a thank-you, refer someone to a friend of mine, or need to write a short note to someone, I use one of our four-color picture postcards. We even include them when we pay our bills. When was the last time someone in the accounts receivable department got a picture of a customer?

I think I can safely promise that you'll see the impact that these special business cards, postcards and memo pads can have on your business building efforts. I know they have made a big difference here at MIM.

Here's one more little idea you can do with your picture. Some people like this idea and some don't. I'll let you decide.

Printers that specialize in printing pressure sensitive labels can take your picture and company name, and provide you rolls of peel-off, stamp-sized labels with your picture and company information on them. You can now stick your picture on every piece of literature that you mail to your prospects. If you like this idea, you can get very creative with it!

Tips And Techniques For Using Business Cards

No matter what you choose to do with your business cards, please don't get the bargain-basement, standard-issue, black-type-on-white card. It's boring. If you're not going to use the four-color picture idea, consider using your photo in a single color instead— or use colored stock for your cards. You can have a designer create a logo for you and layout an artistic, impactful card.

Many printers have inexpensive design services to help you create the unique card you want. Also, if you have a community college or art school in your area, there are many talented students who would jump at the chance to design a card—for a lot less than a professional design firm would charge.

Oh, and make sure to carry a bunch of blank cards with you at all times. Get them done at the same time you have your printed cards made, and do them in some light pastel color.

Why? Because you'll frequently encounter people who don't have a business card with them. It makes a great impression when you can pull out a blank card, hand it to them and say, "I always carry blank cards just in case I meet someone who's been so busy that day that they've given away all their cards." Ask them to write their information on the blank card you've provided so that you can put it in your card deck.

Do you think you've made a positive impression with that person? Will they think that you're a true professional? And even nicer—you didn't embarrass them. You were thoughtful enough to provide them with a card and say that you especially carry them for people who've "given all their cards away that day." I promise, they'll remember you.

Caught Ya!

Okay, what if you're caught without a business card? There you are with the perfect prospect, and no four color cards, no blank cards, nothing. What then? Here's a great idea I used back when I was building my own distributor network. I tried it late one night in a convenience store not far from my home.

I've got a passion. Well, I actually have many of them, but this particular passion is one shared by millions of men and women worldwide. I *love* ice cream.

And, more often than not, my passion for ice cream emerges late at night and sometimes into the wee hours of the morning. So one night when I felt the passion, I hopped into my car and drove down to the 24-hour convenience store.

As you can imagine, I didn't take this late-night journey "dressed for success" in suit and tie. I was "dressed for ice cream"—which, at that time of the night, meant sweats and running shoes. So there I was, standing in line, beloved Swiss-almond-fudge juggling between my hands to keep from melting, and I struck up a conversation with another late-night shopper. We were in rapport in a minute or two, and he agreed to take a look at my opportunity. It was all going perfectly, except for one thing—no business cards!

Fortunately, I always kept a blank business check in my wallet, just for emergencies. It had my company's name, address and phone number on it. So I explained to the gentleman that I was without business cards, but would he mind if I gave him a check? He tilted his head to one side and nodded okay. (I suppose he found me a bit strange.) I made out a check, payable to him for one dollar, and handed it over.

He stared at it. Then looked at me. Then looked back at the check. Then looked at me with a huge grin. Then he told me that this was one of the most amazing things that has ever happened to him!

Necessity is the mother of invention, and this invention really worked well for me. I don't know why people found this so remarkable. And I don't think handing them a dollar bill would have had the same impact. One more thing: of all the checks that I gave out like this, I would estimate that fewer than three out of a hundred *were ever cashed!*

I understand that Picasso never used cash—he always paid by check. His signature was so famous that people would frame his check rather than cash it! Do you suppose they didn't cash my checks for the same reason? Ah, maybe someday.

Check This Out

Here's another way to make checks work for you:

When you get a check for the purchase of products from a retail customer, see if there's anything written on the memo portion of the check. If not—great! Write a short message, a thank-you or something.

"Judy, you're going to love these products!" "Thanks for your confidence, John." If your customer gets checks back with their bank statement, they may see your little message. It only costs you a few seconds, and it can go a long way with people.

Sadly, such thoughtfulness is at a premium in our fast-paced world. Just remember that any effort you make that makes someone feel special gets returned to you a thousand times over.

Be Prepared

The whole point here is to put those business cards— those sharp, polished little tools of yours—*to work.* Remember, you're a walking/talking/living/breathing advertisement for your product and opportunity. Do whatever you can do to be memorable to the people you meet. Keep your name and face familiar to them. Be in the front of their minds when they have the need for a product like yours or when they're considering an opportunity like the one you offer. Anything you can do—*do it*! As I said earlier, there will be times when you'll have only one opportunity to prospect a fortune with a prospect. So be prepared! Have all the tools you'll need ready at a moment's notice—and keep them looking sharp and polished.

Many of the upcoming secrets will give you even more tools to help you build your business: the video or audio pass-out game, your "memory hook," target advertising, a three-step direct mailing program, mastering the telephone and much more.

So get ready to prospect a fortune in Network Marketing. Because by the time you've completed this book, you'll own a toolbox of goodies that will be the envy of the Masters themselves.

And before you dig into the gold mine with the tools from this secret, take a few minutes to complete the Action Steps below. It's a great opportunity to transfer those wonderful ideas in your head onto paper—and then into action!

MY ACTION STEPS

to Mastery of Secret #7:

Master Prospectors use more than a pick and a shovel

Knowing that I need to do this for both myself and for my prospects...

1) Have I done everything possible to look, sound and feel like I'm in business? (Circle one)

Yes or No

2) What more can I do to project a professional image of both myself and my business?

_____

_____

_____

_____

_____

_____

_____

_____

_____

_____

_____

_____

Secret #8

Master Prospectors value time more than money

Did you know that most people place a higher value on their money than they do on their time? Personally, I don't understand that.

If you stop and think about it, we can always make more money. (Of course, if you've never done that successfully, you may have some questions about how it's done.) No matter what we believe about making money—earning it, finding it, borrowing it, having it given to us—we know that it's out there and we can always get more.

But what about time?

Once we spend time, that's it. Just try to get back a year of your life, or even a week. Or how about just *a second*? No way. Time is fleeting. Snap your fingers and it's gone—and gone forever.

No doubt about it, time is the most precious commodity of all. And Master Prospectors value their time above all else. They know it is their single, most valuable asset.

Let's say you want your business to be five times larger than it is today—not only five times the number of people in your network but five times the income as well. You will not accomplish this by spending five times more time on your business. You won't accomplish your goal by working five times harder, either.

If you want five times more success than you have now, you'll need to work five times *smarter* than you are now. And one of the best ways of working smarter in Network Marketing is to make sure that the time you invest with people today is the highest-quality time possible.

Now, notice that I said *invest*. I didn't say spend. There's a very big difference between the two.

Anybody can spend time. In fact, that's what most people are doing this very minute. Spend, spend, spend. No big deal. People say, "I've got all the time in the world."

Wrong!

Time is so precious that we must always be *investing* it. And when you invest your time, why not expect the same high rate of return that you would get from any other investment?

How Much Is Your Time Worth?

Let's say you're a part-time Network Marketer currently earning $1,000 a month. To do this, you invest

15 hours per week (about two or three hours a day for five or six days) building your business. Using your calculator, you'd come up with a value for your efforts of $15.50 per hour (15 hours per week x 4.3 weeks in a month = 64.5 hours ÷ into $1,000 = $15.50 per hour). Not bad for a part-time business in today's economy.

Or is it?

I say you've incorrectly valued your time. I say your time is worth what you *expect to be making one to two years from now.* You see, the work you're doing right now is creating the foundation of the super-successful network you will have in the future.

If your goal is to earn $100,000 a year, working a thirty-hour week with a month's vacation, you're a $70-per-hour person!

If your goal is to keep those same hours and earn $100,000 a month, then you're a $775-per-hour person!

Now how much time can a $775-per-hour person— or for that matter a $70-per-hour person—fritter away with people who aren't interested in his or her opportunity? Or how much time can this highly paid individual spend doing "busy work," instead of making every *very expensive* minute count?

Look, it's your business. You can treat it any way you like. But believe me when I tell you that long before Master Prospectors earned huge bonus checks, they began treating themselves like highly paid professionals earning $70 to $700 per hour. And that's the big reason they earn that kind of money today!

Would you look differently at your daily actions if your hourly rate was $100, $200, or $500 per hour?

Sure you would!

Okay, so here you are, worth a couple of hundred dollars an hour—now what?

Leverage is the key. You need to make your increasingly valuable time *do* five or ten times what it used to. That's how Master Prospectors earn five or ten times more than other Network Marketers—*they do five to ten times more with the time they have to work with.*

And they do it with—you guessed it—more powerful tools. One of which is...

The Awesome Power Of Video

Have you heard the statistics of how many hours of television the average person watches every day? Incredible, isn't it? Adults watch at least three hours a day. Kids and teenagers watch even more than that. No doubt about it, we're a tele-video society. Video rentals are booming, cable TV is exploding, and most people get their news from TV.

Well, the Network Marketing industry is a pioneer in the field of video marketing for a number of very good reasons.

For instance: Put yourself in your prospect's shoes for a moment. He or she is a busy, successful person—just the kind of man or woman you want most in your network. Time is precious to them. You approach them with your business opportunity by inviting them to attend an opportunity meeting for a few hours on a Thursday evening at a local hotel.

You're showing your busy prospect the way you do business. *How open do you think they'll be to the pos-*

sibility of doing a business that takes that much time? I'll answer that for myself—*not very!*

The Video Pass-Out

Let's try another approach:

You call this same busy business person to make an appointment and say, "Ms. or Mr. Hustle-Bustle, I want to stop by your office and introduce myself. I have a money-making opportunity that I'm certain will interest you. I'll need two minutes of your time, and if I take a second longer than that, I promise I will donate $250, in your name, to the charity of your choice. Fair enough?"

Now how would *you* respond to an offer like that— with such a guarantee?

Set up the appointment, show up on time, and after you shake hands, you can say something like:

"Ms. or Mr. Hustle-Bustle, I'm involved in a revolutionary Network Marketing effort that's truly exploding. It's a no-risk opportunity that combines the ability to leverage your time, build a residual income in a matter of months (equal to having hundreds of thousands of dollars in investment assets), provides you with significant tax-saving advantages, and all you have to do is hand a successful, busy person like yourself this sixteen-minute videotape and ask if they'll look at it within twenty-four hours. If what you see on this tape really gets your attention, then we can talk further. Will you look at the tape and let me pick it up from your secretary tomorrow?"

That took forty seconds—and you're out of there with more than a minute to spare.

Now, can you imagine any business that requires such a small time commitment, yet has such enticing and impressive benefits?

And look at the message you're sending this very busy prospect: *This business takes sixty seconds* (plus travel time). More than likely, no "salesperson" has ever approached your prospect like *that* before. Can you imagine how he or she might see that this is something they could do as well, especially if they are a "center of influence" type of person? Would even the busiest person have time for a business that took under two minutes to do?

Friends, used wisely and with the proper prospects, this is powerful!

This method of marketing is called "video pass-out." Depending on your target, you can choose from a wide variety of approaches. You can hand out videos by appointment (as in the example above), or in a chance meeting (just carry a tape or two in your briefcase or bag). You can also do it through the mail—we'll talk more about that later. The point is that no matter how you do it, the message you give to your prospects is that you're involved in the simplest business in the world! Even a busy, successful person can find the time to take a look at it. It's so simple, so easy, and so quick that they'd be foolish not to check it out—right?

Well, that's exactly how thousands of people who've been approached this way have entered a Network Marketing business. The videotape "hooked" their interest to learn more. As they were exposed to more information, people or events—or tried and loved the products—they established enough of a belief system to find (or make) the time necessary to invest in building their business, regardless of how busy they were before. This system works—as long as the person who's working it follows-up and follows-through with every one of their prospects.

Ask For Referrals, Leave The Door Open

If the person cites an objection, such as, "I don't have time to spend sixteen minutes to look at a video," or, "My dog ate my tape player," just say that you understand, and ask if there's a business associate who they know who might be willing to take a look at a tremendous opportunity.

Like I said in Secret #6: **Master Prospectors love to build bridges,** no matter what the outcome, *leave the door open.* Thank the person for his or her time and go away. Make sure you have their address so you can occasionally drop them notes and information. Keep them abreast of your own success and the success of other *busy people* who have joined the business and are doing great in the network. Nothing succeeds like success. Who knows? Perhaps in a month or two your prospect might be more open to taking sixteen minutes to view a video.

What if your company doesn't have a video? That's okay, there are a number of "generic" videos on the market that explain what Network Marketing is all about. Find one that you like and use it.

"I Don't Have A TV"

One possible problem I can see with this approach is that someone may not have a TV. They may not be a TV-watching kind of person, or maybe they don't own a tape player. If that's the case, do the same thing, except use an audio cassette.

Just about everybody has a cassette tape player in their car, and many people find it convenient to soak up their drive-time listening to educational and motivational cassette tapes. Imagine this: You can prospect twenty people some afternoon while you sit at home and they complete their commute. Feels pretty good to be hard at "work" playing with your kids or relaxing by the pool, while your prospects are getting back from the rat race (and easing their pain by listening about your wonderful opportunity for financial and time freedom!). Could you think of a better moment to explain the benefits of your opportunity than to a man or woman stuck in rush-hour traffic?

The key is leverage: how to make all your efforts into E^2 (effort squared). Tapes—both audio and video—are great leveraging tools. Imagine having twenty or thirty audiotapes or videotapes circulating around your town—or even the whole country! Every evening, ten or more people would be watching or listening to your message.

Again, remember: You are the messenger—your job is to get the message out to as many people as possible, and audiotapes and videotapes are two ways to powerfully and consistently spread your message to as many people as possible. You no longer need to rely solely on yourself in one-on-one communication.

Leverage Power

And, please, don't lose sight of one awesome aspect of using these tools: They are absolutely, easily and effortlessly *duplicatable!*

You *could* take all your new distributors and try to teach them how to give compelling personal or public presentations. How long would that take? What would be involved in helping people get over their fears and doubts of public speaking? Or "selling"?

Or you can show your new distributors how to hand their prospects a video or audio cassette tape and how to follow-up. How long would that take? What special talents or abilities does he or she need to be able to do that effectively? And once they find an interested prospect, if they need your abilities to present the total opportunity, you're investing your valuable time with a prospect who's already pre-qualified.

Do you see how quickly anyone could build a network using these powerful leveraging tools?

Here's an important difference between prospectors and Master Prospectors. I ask that you read it twice to make sure it soaks in.

Prospectors value their money more than they do their time. They'll waste their time trying to hold onto their money. *Master Prospectors value their time more than their money.* They'll invest their money into tools that make their time more valuable.

If you're serious about building a highly successful Network Marketing business, please don't waste your time doing it.

Before I close this chapter, I'd like to share with you an article I wrote for *Upline*™—*The Newsletter For Network Marketing Leaders*, in June of 1992. It's entitled *Beyond the Chicken and Egg*, and it addresses a very important point that we discovered while researching the hows and whys of using pros-pecting tools successfully. Here it is:

Beyond The Chicken And Egg

Which comes first—the chicken or the egg?

You know the dilemma: When you want to invite someone to take a look at your Network Marketing business, what do you show them first—your product, or your business plan? Which comes first: the chicken or the egg?

People teach different answers to this question. My answer: *First tell them about farming!* And "farm-ing," of course, is Network Marketing.

Let me explain.

It's important to focus your marketing efforts on the needs of the marketplace—wouldn't you agree? Not on what *you* think is of value, but on what most people out there are looking for.

What do most people need in today's economic cli-mate? Do they need nutritional products, weight-loss products, skin-care products, water-treatment prod-ucts...? The truth is that no matter what a fantastic egg you have—or, for that matter, how great a chicken—neither one is really what most people are looking for.

Today, more than at any other time in our history, what people need most are *financial alternatives*. They need to believe in something that provides them an opportunity to take control of their financial fu-ture. No matter how good your product or how ter-rific your particular business plan, what most people need to hear about first is the opportunity that the *Network Marketing industry itself* offers.

Beyond The "Job"

Even in today's uncertain economy, most people still think about "looking for a job." The first thing we need to do is make a dent in that habitual consciousness by showing them that "a job" is no longer the answer. That, instead, their ongoing success depends on *them*. "Job security" is going the way of the dinosaurs. We need to open their minds to the possibility of working for themselves so they never again have to depend on "a job."

Try introducing them to the concept of taking control of their lives through a marvelous industry called Network Marketing.

The crucial element of this concept is that you're not attempting to "sell" anything here: You're here to *educate*. You can say something like this: "I'm looking for a handful of people who are fed up. People who have gotten to the point where they want to take control of their own future and who are no longer in the market for a job, but an opportunity. There's an industry out there that people need to know about.

"I've got some factual information that explains exactly what this industry is and what it can do for people. I'm not here to try and sell anything: I'm here to inform people about a financial alternative.

"I can share this information with you for a short period of time. I can only allow you to review it for about forty-eight hours because I've got so many other people who want to look it over.

"At the end of those forty-eight hours, if you see a value in it and want to look further at specific possibilities, then I'd love to sit down with you and share some details about the particular products and company I'm involved with. The first step, if you're interested, is to review this generic and factual information about the industry itself."

Why Is This A Good Approach?

For three reasons.

First, because of today's economic climate, it hits most people squarely between the eyes. Being aware of what most people need and want is a quality of Master Prospectors.

Secondly, a lot of people are tired of being sold. They feel they're being sold constantly—on the TV, in the papers, on their phone at dinner time, by the billboards on the freeway... sold, sold, sold. What do you say we try to give them a break?

If you're attracted to this secret, try taking a percentage of the people you meet and using this strategy—not everyone, just try it with a few prospects to see how they react. Don't try to *sell* these people on anything. Let them know right up front—that there are no strings attached to your offer to educate them. Then *you* be the judge as to how well this approach works for you.

The third (and possibly the strongest) reason for this approach is that you connect your prospect to the big picture *first*. You increase your percentages of finding people who first connect to the process of Network Marketing. And the best business builders in

Network Marketing today are the ones who love the process.

Then, when you sit down to "sell" them on the specifics of your products and company—they're already "sold"! When they connect to the possibilities of the process, they'll have a sense (subconsciously, if nothing else) that they want your products and specific opportunity to work for them. They'll end up selling themselves on your gift.

Are You Creating A Positive Belief System?

Yes and no. In a sense, you're helping create a positive belief with people who *want* to have that belief. But you're not really creating it—if anything, you're unleashing a positive belief system that was *waiting to be born.* You're tapping into people's desire for an alternative and showing them a solution. You're giving them hope and finding out which people are ready to make a change—and which people are not.

Remember—and this is important—*you're not trying to convince people of the value of Network Marketing!* You're aware of the economic climate, and you know that they are, too. You're coming from a place of pure contribution—not "pretending" to do so—but *really* doing so. You're letting this information get into their hands, and then they will make a choice whether or not they want to look into it further.

If, after reviewing your information, they're not open to the financial alternative of Network Marketing, nothing prevents you from still sharing your products with them—*so you've lost nothing.* Just make sure to get your prospecting tools back so you can share them with the next person. And if they *are* open to looking at the opportunity within Network Marketing, then by first connecting them to the process, you've increased your chances of sponsoring a real business builder—not simply a wholesale product user.

What Kind Of Tools?

Complimentary to this approach is the idea of using "generic" tools—information that educates and inspires people about the industry of Network Marketing. The more generic the information—the more they'll see it as information, not sales literature.

Today there are a good number of generic tools available. Some people use pamphlets or books, others use audio tapes, and still others like to rely on videos. What's the most effective approach?

I believe in using two tools because there are two different needs you want fulfill: to inspire and to inform.

First Inspire—Then Inform

It's been proven that the *written word* is one of the most powerful ways to give people facts—to *inform* them.

When people see something in print, they're more likely to believe it. Using a good pamphlet or book on Network Marketing to convey solid, professional information about the industry lends more credibility.

But no matter how good or how interesting the book is, some people will not invest the time to sit down and read it unless their interest is already piqued. So you can also share with them a tool that will compel them *emotionally* to read the book—and the medium of *video or audio tape* is perfectly suited for that purpose.

A video is a powerful way to tap people's emotions—not their logic, their emotion. To some extent, an audio tape can do that as well. An audio, however does not convey images as powerfully as a good video; on the other hand, it can be listened to in the car, and doesn't require that the person set aside the short time it takes to sit down in their living room to view it. So both video and audio tapes have their strong points. It's a personal thing as to which you prefer to use.

By using tools like these—video or audio tapes and a book—you can have the greatest impact. You've improved your chances tremendously of getting into your prospect's mind and showing them that this is a viable business opportunity.

At Millionaires in Motion, for example, we've created an entire family of generic prospecting tools: a brief, easy to read book on what Network Marketing is and what it is not; a short, yet powerful video and audio tape; and an attention getting pamphlet. They're all designed to complement each other in educating your prospects. We call them "The Greatest Opportunity in the History of the World Family of Prospecting Tools." See the Resource Center at the back of this book for more details.

If your Network Marketing company or upline has produced tools designed to assist you in prospecting *business builders*, and in using them you find that they work—then use them as often as you can, especially if they are designed to educate your prospect in Network Marketing.

The Process Is The Product

Remember that the most successful people in Network Marketing are those who love the industry as much as—if not more than—their own company. As I said earlier, they love the process. Consequently, they push through all adversity and any disappointment or discouragements they may encounter. They're the ones who become hugely successful in this industry. Why? Because they *never* give up on the industry.

What better way to introduce someone to Network Marketing than to share with them the process itself—before you show them the chicken *or* the egg!

Yes, your time is the most valuable asset that you and your business possess. What is your time worth today? What do you want it to be worth a year from today? Use the following Action Steps to help you move from where you are now to where you want to be.

MY ACTION STEPS

to Mastery of Secret #8:

Master Prospectors value
time more than money

1) What is the current, estimated *hourly* income that
    I earn with my business?

(_____) ÷ (_____) = $_____
   my monthly income   hours worked   hourly rate
                            per month

2) How many hours a month do I see myself devot-
    ing to my business twelve months from now?

    _____ (hours per month)

3) What hourly income do I want my business to be
    providing me in twelve months?

    $_____ (per hour)

4) What company, upline or generic prospecting
    tools can I invest in today that will make my time
    more productive and my twelve-month income
    goals a reality?

    _____

    _____

    _____

    _____

    _____

_____

_____

_____

_____

_____

_____

_____

_____

Secret #9

Master Prospectors know every business needs an S.O.B.

---

*N*ow, what do you suppose I mean by, "Every business needs an S.O.B."?

The S.O.B. I'm talking about stands for "Statement Of Benefit," and it is perhaps one of the most powerful tools in the toolbox of the Master Prospectors!

Statement Of Benefit

Last year I attended a conference on a chartered cruise ship that went from San Diego to Mexico and back. There were a number of terrific speakers on board as part of the program. One of the speakers really got my attention—he was an expert on the art of Networking.

One of the concepts that truly interested me was something that he called "a memory hook." You use it when you're introduced to someone and it's designed to make that person highly curious about who you are and what you do. It "hooks" them into asking you questions so they can learn more about you. He gave us examples of memory hooks that use people's names or the name of their companies. I saw the *true* value of the memory hook when he spoke about using it to communicate a benefit that you or your business offers people.

Can you see how powerful and useful this would be in your prospecting efforts? I did, and I leaned forward on my chair, listening intently to what the speaker was saying.

All of a sudden, I realized exactly what a memory hook was and how it worked! There I was, *hooked;* leaning forward on my chair, focusing all my attention on the speaker and what he was about to say. I was more than curious—I wanted to hear *every word.* Why? Because I wanted the benefit that he was offering. The "hook" he used to describe the "memory hook" had gotten me curious and involved.

The speaker then gave us an exercise. We each created our own S.O.B. Then all of us mingled and introduced ourselves to each other using our own memory hook.

One woman was the accounts receivable manager for a Network Marketing service company called Business Applications Group—or BAG, for short. She introduced herself by saying, "Hi, I'm Sally, the nag from BAG. I get the money, honey."

Another woman, an independent distributor whose name was Pepper, said, "Hello, my name is Pepper. My business puts spice in people's lives."

I thought both of those were pretty cute. They got my attention and made me curious to know more about the two women and their businesses. But the S.O.B. really sank in when a man named Buddy, a financial planner, introduced himself to me.

Now I've met many financial planners, and over the years—right or wrong—I've developed a picture of what a financial planner looks like and does. Kind of accountant-like, not very exciting or creative, and I've always thought I knew more about planning for my financial future than they did. So if Buddy had come up to me and said, "Hi, I'm Buddy, and I'm a financial planner," I would have probably made some small-talk and moved on quickly so I could chat with someone else.

But Buddy's approach *really* got my attention. He "hooked" me!

We introduced ourselves and I asked him, "So, Buddy, what do you do for a living?" And Buddy said, "Well, John, my clients say I make them free of financial worries for the rest of their lives."

Hello, Buddy. Can we talk?

Do you see how Buddy didn't tell me about something that I didn't care about? He didn't brag and talk about how great he was. He just told me what his clients said about him. It was very smart of him to get that third-party endorsement in there. And what they said about what Buddy provided them was a benefit just about everybody I know would be interested in— including me. That's a *perfect* memory hook. That's a powerful S.O.B. That's one of the reasons why Buddy is my financial planner today!

Positioning Is The Key

Positioning is one of the most powerful marketing concepts of all. How you position yourself and your Network Marketing opportunity in the marketplace can make or break your enterprise.

And the key to successful positioning is *benefits*.

Every business wants to create a position in the mind of its current and potential customers—a posture that is memorable and stands out from all the rest. A business that states a clear and compelling S.O.B. can attract the greatest number of people.

The concept of positioning came from the advertising gurus of Madison Avenue. Advertising people know that they have two seconds or less to get people's attention in an ad, or with a product on the store shelf. If they don't create a successful position in the mind of the consumer, someone else will. And that "someone else" will get the business.

Many people think that the *top* position is the *only* position. That's not always the case.

Do you remember when the upstart car rental agency Avis advertised, "We're number two. We try harder"? Hertz is still number one, but Avis separated itself from all other car rental companies and took sole possession of that lucrative number two spot. They were Masters of positioning.

Another example is a product called "Shake 'n' Bake." They managed to get their S.O.B. right in their name! The words "Shake 'n' Bake" say "easy" and "fun to use." The company even added a tagline: "Fried chicken flavor without the mess." Boy, did that hit home.

See, it's not the best overall position that counts. It's the best position for the people you're talking to. The position you want is something unique... something no one else offers... something that directly appeals to what people want most.

So what position do you want for your business? How will you "hook" your prospects into wanting to know more about what you do? What S.O.B.—Statement Of Benefit—will you communicate to them?

Write down, in the space below, a couple of possible S.O.Bs that you feel are the hottest hot-buttons you have to offer people—using either your product or your opportunity.

_____

_____

_____

_____

_____

_____

_____

Now why is all this positioning and S.O.B. stuff so important?

Do you remember when we were talking about business cards? I said that in Network Marketing, you're *paid to advertise!*

One common mistake that unsuccessful distributors make in this business is that they advertise the wrong thing. They're so busy giving people all the features of their product or opportunity—the ingredients of the product or all the details of the business plan—that they miss the most important communication of all—*the benefits.*

The Benefits Of Benefits

Benefits get people's attention. Benefits are what people want most from you.

How you communicate the benefits to people can mean the difference between success or failure in your business.

The reason you build rapport and learn about what people need and want is so you can tailor your *benefits* specifically *for them.* Simply put, people want to know *what's in it for them.* That means *benefits.*

Do you know how many ½-inch drill bits are sold in America every year? Millions, and sales continue to grow every year. And do you know what's really amazing? Not one of those people wanted a ½-inch drill bit. *They all wanted ½-inch holes!*

The drill bit is the means to an end. What people want is the *benefit* they get from the drill bit. And it's the same with Network Marketing products or opportunities.

People don't want to take vitamins—they want to feel vital, healthy and alive!

People don't want to smear skin-care products on their faces—they want to look ten years younger!

People don't want a business opportunity—they want more control of their life and work. They want to invest more time with their families. They want the freedom to travel and be adventurous. People want to have more fun!

And here's an important one: *People don't want more money—they want the benefits that come from having more money.* They want what money will buy them—a house, a new car, free time, security, retirement, paying for college....

The more you focus your efforts on communicating clear, instantly recognized and highly valued benefits to all the people you come in contact with—the more successful you'll become in this business. Master Prospectors know this.

Do you know what Master Prospectors do all day? They tell people about ½-inch holes.

They communicate benefits every time they open their mouths. Every communication they make—every phone call, every button, business card, letter or package they send out—is covered with Statements Of Benefit.

Gives a whole new meaning to a S.O.B.—wouldn't you agree?

Bring the S.O.B. you created on page 143 one step closer to reality by completing your Action Steps on the following page.

MY ACTION STEPS

to Mastery of Secret #9:

Master Prospectors know every business needs an S.O.B.

Before you begin this exercise, I want you to imagine this: every time someone asks you, "What do you do?" they are giving you permission to show them your fifteen-second commercial. For a few moments you have their undivided attention and interest—you have their approval to advertise. If your commercial cost you thousands of dollars to produce, you would know *exactly* what it would look like and *exactly* what it would say.

1) So, with that in mind, what S.O.B. (Statement of Benefit) will you communicate to your prospects? How will your commercial "hook" them into wanting to know more about your business?

_____

_____

_____

_____

_____

_____

_____

_____

_____

_____

_____

Secret #10

Master Prospectors don't like to cut down trees

---

*H*ere's an important difference between Master Prospectors and everybody else in Network Marketing: The more Master Prospectors know, the less they say.

Funny, isn't it? Most people spend all their time amassing more and more knowledge so they can have all the answers—and then they want to give it to a prospect *all at once.*

Well, *that doesn't work!*

I don't know where people get the idea that burying a prospect under a mountain of information will get that person interested. I've watched distributors do this over and over again. They'll be making a presentation to a prospect, and every time the prospect asks a question, they run back to their briefcase or bag and pull out another stack of stuff. Then with an excited, "Look at all of this!," they proceed to dump another truckload of material on top of their prospect.

I guess they were taught, "When in doubt, hand out more handouts."

That's why I say that Master Prospectors don't like to cut down trees. Can you imagine how many stately hundred-year-old trees go into all that paper? And really, how much of it gets used? How much of it gets trashed?

It's true that, "The more people you tell, the more you sell." It's equally true that, "The less you say, the more people want to know."

It's About Building Expectations

I'm sure you've seen the previews of coming attractions in a movie theater. How long do you think they last—a couple of minutes or so? They're that short so you'll want to see the whole movie. It's a taste—that's all. A tantalizing taste which promises that the best is yet to come.

Master Prospectors do the same thing. They don't spill their candy in the lobby. They like to hand it out a little at a time. They like to engage people's natural curiosity. When they give a little, the result is an even greater desire from their prospects to know more... and then *more*... and *still more*.

This is especially true when Master Prospectors are communicating through the mail.

Sending information to prospects via mail or parcel post is a vital part of building a highly successful, national or global Network Marketing business.

Too many distributors try to cram envelopes chock-full of loose pages, flyers, booklets and brochures about their product and business plan. They zip it off via priority mail, and two days later the prospect gets an avalanche of reading material— right along with all the other catalogs, junk mail and bills that everyone else is sending them.

Who has the time to read all that stuff? Do you? And what does that procedure tell your prospect about how the business is done?

Yes, we *do* need to send information and products through the mail. The key lies in the *quality* of what we send, not the *quantity*.

Using The Mail To Prospect

Although I am a big supporter of effective use of the mail, I do not recommend using *only* direct mail to build your Network Marketing business.

Direct mail is serious business. Some of the highest-paid, most successful marketing professionals in the world have made their fortunes in direct mail. It's an art and a science, and in order to do it successfully, you'll need to invest considerable resources. You also better know what you're doing.

Most people do not. And many Network Marketing hopefuls have lost their shirts because they dumped good-sized chunks of money and time into poorly organized direct-mail campaigns.

Yet there are ways to use a direct-mail approach that will help you avoid costly mistakes and will also substantially increase your odds for success. Let me tell you what a friend of mine did.

A Direct Mail Approach That *Really* Works

When my friend—we'll call him Jim—got into Network Marketing, he knew he didn't want to conduct meetings. He didn't have time to run around town making one-on-one presentations either. Jim was a well-respected consultant in the natural health field, so there were many people around the country who knew him and trusted him. He had a reputation for quality and integrity.

Jim started by making a list of 160 people. He wrote a four-page letter in classic direct-mail style telling people about the benefits he'd received from using these unique Network Marketed products. He included a lot of third-party testimonials as well: about half of the letter included personal stories from satisfied customers.

At the end of his letter, Jim asked people to try the products *risk-free*. He wrote that he believed so strongly that they would see and feel a difference in their health, vitality and mental clarity that he was willing to offer a complete money-back guarantee. "Try these products for twenty-eight days," he said, "and if you don't get the results I promise, I'll return your money in full."

He included a brochure that told the recipient about the unique qualities of the products; how they were grown, harvested, and packaged, and also a detailed description of their nutritional composition.

Jim then took a three-step approach:

The Three-Step Direct Mail Approach

First, he called the people on his list and told them about the fantastic products he'd recently discovered. (To fully prepare himself, he outlined a script that would clearly communicate stories of benefit to his prospects.) His enthusiasm, energy, and belief in the products was persuasive and contagious. He asked if they'd be interested in receiving some information. If they said, "Yes," and they promised to read it and not throw it away, he told them that he would send it out immediately. All he wanted was for them to take a look at his letter. No strings. No sales pitch. Just "look it over."

Now he didn't call everybody at once. He made a commitment to make four calls every weekday plus Saturday until he'd been through his entire list.

Because of his enthusiasm, his reputation and his center-of-influence, just about everybody agreed to look at his letter.

Living up to his commitment, he sent out four letters every day. That was his **second** step.

At the end of the letter, Jim wrote that he'd call them in a day or two—unless, of course, they called him first. He also included a special note after his signature which said that if they were excited about the products and thought that they knew four other people that would like to try them, he could show them how they could get their products *free.* Many of the people he mailed letters to were excited enough to call him before he called them.

In his follow-up call (his **third** step), he would ask, "Did you read the letter?" If they hadn't, he asked them when they could and made a date to call them back. If they had read the letter, he would ask, "What was the one thing that interested you the most about the products?" He would tell them more about that specific feature, always ending with a story of benefit from his own experience, or the great results that someone else was getting.

Finally, he would ask his prospect if they wanted to try the products. He offered to help them select the products that were best suited for their particular needs and wants. He chose not to bring up anything about the opportunity, about becoming a wholesale consumer, or how to get their products free—*unless they asked.*

Once again, here's the process: 1) Call and get a commitment to read the letter. 2) Send the letter. 3) Follow up with a phone call. Every day Jim made four calls—either introduction or follow-up calls or a combination of the two.

Jim got extraordinary results. Out of 160 people on his list, *over 130 of them agreed to try the products!*

His business was cash-based, so his customers paid for the products up front. Jim didn't want to have to pay for a substantial inventory, and his company was willing to ship directly to the customer. So he passed most of the orders straight to the company and they drop-shipped the orders for him.

The Follow-Up

A few days after his customers received the products, Jim would call again. He'd tell them the best way to take the products in a kind of "post-selling" job that would keep them excited and expecting great

results. He'd call back one week after they started using the products and again two weeks after they began—both times just to see how they felt. He'd answer all of their questions, and of course, close each
conversation with another story of benefit. He
wanted to be sure that they would continue using the
products so they'd get the results he promised.

Twenty-eight days after they'd begun to use the
products, Jim would call them up and remind them of
the money-back guarantee. Four people said they experienced no results and wanted their money back.
This was no problem—Jim simply got a credit from
his company. A number of people who didn't see all of
the results they wanted agreed to continue to try the
products for another month—again, with a money-
back guarantee. Of that group, four more never got
results and asked for their money back. Jim's total
returns amounted to only six percent of all the people
who originally purchased the products.

Once people used the products and enjoyed the results, they were "sold" on them. Jim would then explain to them how they could get free product for
themselves by sharing the product successfully with
four other people. This way he got good, quality referrals to continue his calling and mailing system. He
never ran out of qualified names to work his three-
step approach.

Some people he invited to become wholesale distributors. To others he offered the business opportunity. All the while, he continued to work his list and
use his three-step approach.

In the end, out of 160 prospects, Jim sponsored
thirty-five new distributors. He created a retail base
that generated more than $500 net profit per month

(not including his bonus check from the company), and in only three months he was on his way to fame and fortune in his Network Marketing business.

The *Negative* Power Of Duplication

One very powerful aspect of this three-step process is how duplicatable it can be. Now, I say "can," because it can work *for* you or *against* you.

As successful as Jim was with his three-step approach, it began to fall apart for him because he didn't make it duplicatable for his people. Let me explain.

Jim was a marketing consultant. He'd been writing "sales" copy for years. He was also a nationally respected figure in the natural foods industry, and that's a strong "center-of-influence" position to come from. Jim also had $20,000 worth of desktop publishing equipment at his finger tips that he used to produce the letters and mailing packets.

With all of this going for him, Jim's success was not surprising. Unfortunately, the people that Jim brought into the business couldn't match his writing ability, industry recognition and respect, and computer expertise.

Simply put, the people Jim brought into the business weren't able to duplicate his success. His success was unique to him. The only business-builders Jim was likely to attract and duplicate himself with were people just like him. People with similar talents, reputations, and resources.

And that's the challenge with the direct-mail approach to Network Marketing. Remember, this is the duplication business. If you're going to use the mail to prospect and promote your products, you've got to set it up so that your people can do the same thing.

The Three-Step Mailing Approach is a great idea and it *works!*

The most important things to remember are:

1) Work with your own name list and referrals from the people on it. It's called "relationship marketing." You can dramatically raise the odds of success in your favor by contacting people or referrals from people who you already know.

2) Avoid dumping information and offers on your prospects. Focus on telling stories. When you mail information, stick to the highlights and give details only as needed or requested.

3) The money-back guarantee is most important. Stores don't offer this kind of no-risk trial. It's a great selling feature.

4) Above all, make it duplicatable for *everybody*. Design your letters and offers so that they can be used by all the new distributors you bring into the business.

The mail can be a powerful ally. Make it an extension of your person-to-person business. Make your mailings into a duplicatable system for all your people and you'll have a tremendous tool for creating near-instant Master Prospectors.

If you'd like to use the mail to promote your business, try this proven three-step approach. Not only will you improve your chances of duplicating yourself, you'll improve the environment by saving a tree!

This approach may not be for everyone, but if it ignites a spark within you, turn it into a fire! You can start by completing the Action Steps that follow.

MY ACTION STEPS

to Mastery of Secret #10:

Master Prospectors don't like to cut down trees

1) If I decide to use the Three-Step Mailing Approach to help me build my business, how many people do I agree to call every day (or every week)? For how long or for how many people? (Write out your agreement with yourself in the space below.)

_____

_____

_____

_____

_____

_____

_____

_____

_____

_____

2) What items will I need to create and organize to get started? (List items such as: mailing list, product and/or opportunity offering, direct-mail letter, brochure, phone script, follow-up system, and so on.)

Items for step #1: *The phone calls*

_____

_____

_____

_____

_____

_____

_____

_____

Items for step #2: *The mailings*

_____

_____

_____

_____

_____

_____

_____

_____

Items for Step #3: *The follow-up*

_____

_____

_____

_____

_____

_____

_____

_____

_____

Secret #11

Master Prospectors have 250-pound friends

---

*I*t's amazing how many people in this business have phones that weigh 250 pounds! Most people have a difficult time picking up a phone that weighs that much. How about you?

Of course, there are people who seem at home with a phone in their hands, just like there are people who are natural prospectors. Most of us, however, have to practice these things in order to master them.

It's been proven that the telephone is one of the most powerful tools of a Master Prospector. How else can you "reach out and touch *any*one" no matter how far away they live and work? If you want to become a Master Prospector, you need to make the phone your friend.

Do Not Disturb!

I'm lucky. I never had to learn to become friends with my phone. I love to talk and the phone has been an incredible blessing. Although I prefer looking eye-to-eye while talking, it's okay, because the telephone allows me to be with many more people.

However, I relate to *writing* in much the same way as some people do to using the phone.

Sometimes when I'd sit down to write, my hand would feel like it weighed 250 pounds. I'd sit there for twenty minutes or so, trying to clear my mind of all kinds of stuff. Upcoming projects and unfinished items would race through my head. My mind would get cluttered with everything *except* what I was trying to write about, and what's worse is that I'd *let it!*

And if that wasn't enough, I was "attacked" by outside forces. The phone would ring, people would come into my office and talk... you name it, it happened. Then one day I got fed up. I became determined that I would learn how to focus on writing and get comfortable with it. So I hung a "do not disturb" sign on my door, put the phone and all the people trying to reach me on "hold," and refused to be interrupted.

No, I couldn't put my mind on "hold." It still continued to chatter about this and that, but I'd learned long ago how to manage my mind. So I took charge and started writing.

The first time I tried this it worked incredibly well. I wrote more in a two-hour session than I had in a week. After a warm-up period—maybe twenty minutes or so—I began to experience the "flow." You know the flow I'm talking about. Your mind clears, your thought process starts to focus on the task at hand and the creative juices begin to *flow* onto the paper.

What a great feeling! You don't want to stop when you're in the flow, do you? It might take time and patience to get there, but when you do, *wow!*

That's how I trained myself to write, and it's also a way that you can become effective and comfortable with your phone.

First, set aside a block of time for the phone, the whole phone and nothing but the phone—so help you! Then put out the "do not disturb" sign to the world. Clear your mind and get down (or up) to business. Let yourself get into "the flow."

Phone-Sense And Nonsense

A taxi driver needs an automobile. A cowboy needs a gun. An actor needs a stage. And a Network Marketer needs a phone.

Can you imagine a cabbie borrowing someone else's car every time he or she had a fare? How about Cowboy Pete challenging Black Bart at high noon, and just before facing the notorious outlaw, he turns to the crowd and asks, "Oh, excuse me, does anybody have a gun I could use?"

Wrong!

I suggest that you have a phone of your own and a place set aside for your home-based business. And I don't mean the kitchen table! Sometimes? Sure, but it's not an office—not even a home office. So set aside a place for you and your phone.

Also, look into getting a two-line phone and two phone lines; one incoming, one outgoing. Publish, in the phone book and on your stationary and business cards, only the number of the incoming line. This lets you make all the calls you want on your outgoing line undisturbed.

This brings me to a pet peeve of mine: call-waiting.

I get by far the biggest cheers and applause in my seminars when I say, "If you have call-waiting, *blow it up!*" People love it! Why? Because *nearly everyone's* phone conversations have been disrupted by this annoying technological advance.

I've partnered many projects with a dear friend and business associate of mine, John Fogg, the editor of *Upline*™ newsletter. John lives in North Carolina and I'm in California, about 3000 miles away. As you can imagine, we work a lot over the phone. In fact, we had spent literally hundreds of hours together on the phone without ever having met each other face-to-face! It's only been recently that we've met in person.

John is a very considerate and thoughtful man. That's probably why he put call-waiting on his phone in the first place—he didn't want anyone to *not* get through.

We'd be on the phone, talking and brainstorming some part of a book or article and really getting into it, when all of a sudden—*click...click*—and John would ask me to please hold for a moment, he had another call. In the course of an hour-long conversation, this could happen as many as six or seven times. John's a busy guy. Lots of people wanted to talk to him—well, *so did I!*

Have you ever been on a hot creative streak and had it abruptly halted? You know, put on hold, sitting there with your mouth half-open, waiting and trying to keep your thought?

Now don't think for a moment that I'm getting revenge on John by saying this. It bothers him, too, and he's constantly apologizing to me. In fact, when I told him I was writing about this in my new book, but I wouldn't use his name, he said, "Go ahead, John—use it. It's true. It's rude and thoughtless of me—and it drives me nuts, too! You're right, I should blow up my call-waiting!"

In The Now

I try very hard to "be here now." I make no claims of Mastery, but I am convinced of the value of being fully present with people, whether on the phone with them or in person. When you give your undivided attention, you get the most from an interaction. Interrupting phone conversations is not only unprofessional; it also saps focus, cuts flow, minimizes results and makes the call a struggle.

The answer: two phone lines, one coming in and one going out. Since you shouldn't make an outgoing call over the incoming line—and you don't have to give out your outgoing number to anyone—that incoming line is very inexpensive. You only pay the minimum monthly charge and you don't need any of the fancy services. And since it's a dedicated business line, you always know what the call is about.

Get an answering machine or a voice mailbox connected to that incoming line, so when you're in a "calling mode," you won't be disturbed—and you won't miss any important calls.

Set aside a block of time you're willing to devote each and every day to phone calls: rapport building calls, setting appointments, follow-up, and so on. Stick to that time and make it a daily habit. *There is no more powerful action you can take to become a Master Prospector and generate great success for your Networking business than to diligently make calls every day.*

Organization And Preparation Is The Key

Master Prospectors are Masters of organization and preparation. They're all "Boy Scouts" and "Girl Scouts" at heart, because they're always prepared. They create systems and support structures that handle all of the details of their business building. The direct effect is that they stay right on track; the precessional effect (Secret #1) is that they unleash their creativity. They can focus on the *personal relationships* that are at the heart of their Networking business.

Here are a couple of secrets within a secret:

The Manager In A Box is a simple yet powerful system that organizes your prospecting and follow-up efforts. If you don't already have a good follow-up system, here's a winner!

Get a 3x5 card file box, a pack or two of 3x5 cards, and numbered dividers for every day of the month. Every prospect gets a card that lists all of their vital information—name, phone number, their expectations, what products or materials you sent them and details of your last phone conversation. (If you like to write a lot, you might want to use 4x6 cards!)

Every time you contact a prospect, have their card in front of you. Make notes about the call, log the date when you agreed to call them next, and put the card behind that day's divider in the box. Then, every morning (or whatever time you've set aside to make your calls), pull out all the cards for that day and set them in front of you. You're completely organized. All the information you need is right at your finger-tips. As the highly successful advertisement says, "The system is the solution."

I can't tell you how many Network Marketing Master Prospectors still rely on this simple little "manager in a box," to keep them on track and successful. The more sophisticated Masters are using contact management software on their computers to stay on top of their follow-up!

Phone Scripts are incredibly useful tools that work for beginners and seasoned Master Prospectors alike. Let me explain how they work with my own story:

When I first began to lead training seminars, I worked from fully detailed scripts. I would write out my entire talk, practice it word for word in front of a mirror, tape and play it over and over again in my car.

When I gave a presentation, I recited nearly every word on that script. Sometimes, when I'd forget a passage or point, I'd consult my notes and actually read from the script until I got back on track.

I did this because I was scared to death of public speaking. My biggest fear was standing there, saying nothing, and everyone knowing that I'd forgotten. The script served as my security blanket.

As I became more comfortable and confident, I trimmed the script so that only the key points were outlined. Then I graduated to having only a topic outline in front of me. And now, I'm so familiar and comfortable with my style and subject that I rarely use notes at all.

So if you're concerned about what you're going to say to prospects, I'd recommend you approach your telephone efforts the same way.

Work with your upline sponsor and put together complete scripts for different telephone interactions: setting appointments, building rapport, follow-up, and so on. Focus on the questions you're going to ask your prospect—remember, it's better for you to do less talking and your prospect to do more.

Once you get a handle on your phone conversations, cut back to using just an outline or a list of key questions. I know many Master Prospectors who— even after years of phone-calling—keep a list of questions in front of them every time they call.

Power Up Your Phone Space/Work Station with positive reinforcements. Use motivational pictures and quotes to constantly remind you of your goals. Put them all around so you can see them while you're using the phone. Paste up reminders of the qualities you want to have or be. Notes like "Smile!" and key questions to ask your prospects or business associates are also great.

One Master Prospector I know has this reminder right in front of him on his desk: "What are you committed to right now?" He says that this keeps him focused on his commitment to the people he's talking to and reminds him that the call is not about him—it's about *them*.

A mirror is a powerful tool to have in front of you when you're making calls. Not only can you check your enthusiasm level, but seeing yourself "as others see you" brings a new dimension to your phone skills.

Limiting The Time of Your Calls is another powerful support structure. I know many Master Prospectors who get on the phone to set an appointment with a prospect and turn over a simple three-minute egg timer as soon as they say "hello." They know that if they haven't gotten an appointment in three minutes, more than likely they're not getting one—at least not on that day. So, when three minutes are up, they move on.

Three minutes might be too little time for someone just starting out, but ten minutes is plenty. Setting and sticking to a strict time limit will dramatically increase your telephone productivity.

And do what works. There's always that time when a twenty-minute call can really empower your prospect. So do your best to make and keep time limits, yet be sensitive to what the other person needs and wants. Remember that the purpose of time limits is to keep you as productive as you can possibly be.

Make sure you're happy with your furnishings and equipment. You're going to be investing lots of time in this work station/telephone office of yours, so make it a point to set it up in a way that pleases you and truly supports you.

A card table and a straight-backed folding metal chair probably won't cut it. Get a chair you like and the kind of phone that you really want. Have the area appointed in a way that brings out your best.

No, I'm not advising you to go deep into debt buying a solid, hand-carved mahogany desk and a $2,700 massage recliner. I *am* recommending that you equip your home office with the most comfortable and attractive furnishings you can acquire. *This is your place of business. Imagine how productive you'd be if you truly enjoyed being there!*

Your telephone especially needs to appeal to you, both visually and functionally. Nowadays, you can get phones in a wide variety of shapes and sizes with an extraordinary number of features. Cartoon-character phones, cordless phones, headset phones, speaker phones, speed-dialing phones, even picture phones! The point is to get what you like and can afford. The environment you create is not an expense— it's an investment in your success.

Remember: Create a work space that you enjoy and feel good about. Your success depends on it.

Apply these principles and you'll turn that 250-pound phone into a light-'n'-bright balloon of a thing that you'll use with confidence and ease. It's been said that confidence comes from competence. Well, the only way to make a friend out of your 250-pound phone is to become so comfortable and competent with it that it soon becomes as light as a feather.

Every Master Prospector I know has mastered the phone and every Master Prospector's phone is one of their best friends!

———————

I hope your pen doesn't weigh 250 pounds, because you'll need it to complete the following Action Steps. Please do them now!

MY ACTION STEPS

to Mastery of Secret #11:

Master Prospectors have 250-pound friends

1) The following is a list of things I can do to make my phone one of my best friends.

   Phone skills I want to develop and master:

   _____

   _____

   _____

   _____

   _____

   _____

   _____

   _____

   _____

   Things I need (or need to do) to create the ideal work station environment for my home or office:

   _____

   _____

_____

_____

_____

_____

_____

_____

_____

Support structures I would like to put in place to help me *master* the phone:

_____

_____

_____

_____

_____

_____

_____

_____

_____

Secret #12

————

Master Prospectors
live in the future—today!

————

Do you like science fiction? Star Trek, movies and books about the future? I do. I love them. Not because they're simply escapist fun, but because many of the things they talk about are coming true!

Do you remember when you saw your first science fiction movie or TV show where computers talked back to people? Well, today you can walk down to the computer store and buy one that does just that!

Technology is changing our lives so fast today that what once took fifty years to change we accomplish today in only five. It's true! Do you know that more than eighty percent of the things we use almost every day didn't even exist when most of us were born?

Think about it: at the end of the Second World War there were no videotape players. No TVs. No direct dialing. No answering machines. No electronic type-writers. No photocopying machines. No hand-held hair dryers. No dental floss. No velcro. No fast food restaurants or franchises of any kind. No credit cards. No digital watches. No Frisbees. No running shoes. No malls. No suburbs. No commercial jet travel. No automatic washing machines. No aspirin. No x-ray machines. No fax machines. No mutual funds. No Disneyworld. No ballpoint pens. No paper towels. No calculators. No Kleenex. No penicillin. No disposable diapers. No daycare centers. No twist-off bottle caps. No contact lenses. The list goes on.

Amazing, isn't it?

Now, how would you like to be one of the pioneers who brings tomorrow's technology back from the future into practical daily use today? Would that be both exciting and profitable to you?

Well, guess what? *You are a pioneer!*

Why? Because you are a member of one of the most technologically advanced industries in the world—Network Marketing. Sound a little boastful, you say? Wishful thinking? Not at all. Here's proof:

Do you know of any other industry that has made more extensive use of video marketing—using video tapes to prospect and market products?

Network Marketing companies and their independent distributors use more videos to promote their wares than probably any other industry *in the world.*

I know one Networking company that had gross sales of $70 million, and *$20 million of that was video-tapes!*

Another company was growing quite nicely with over 50,000 distributors and annual sales in excess of $100 million. They produced two powerful videotapes and priced them so low that virtually every new distributor could have twenty or thirty of them to play the video pass-out game (Secret #8). In less than two years, this company was close to their goals of 200,000 distributors and $500 million in sales!

Coincidence? I don't think so.

Did you know that the very existence of Network Marketing is based on computer technology?

Without the computer, there wouldn't be a Network Marketing industry as we know it today.

Imagine tracking a modest network of 10,000 distributors; figuring commission checks and sending them out accurately and on time; taking and processing orders; keeping track of inventory... all without the computer. No way! How about trying to do all of that with 100,000 distributors, or *two million distributors* (like industry leader Amway) throughout the world!

Since the mid-1970s, Network Marketing's compelling need for advanced computer technology enabled our industry to grow with giant steps.

Do you know of any other industry that has made such innovative use of teleconferencing and conference calling?

What other business brings over one thousand people together for a phone meeting to share product and opportunity success stories? Network Marketing was probably the first industry in the world to have a thousand-person conference call! Every week, tens of thousands of people around the world attend opportunity meetings and distributor trainings from the comfort of their own homes, via Network Marketing-sponsored teleconferences.

Who else could do a month-end sales push with a series of conference calls that generated a $40 million sales volume *in only three days!* And, by the way, it wasn't a company that created that—it was an individual distributor and his network leaders!

With conference calling, the busiest Master Prospectors with the most demanding schedules can leverage their valuable time by reaching hundreds of people with just one phone call. Prospects can hear enthusiastic personal testimonials from men and women with a wide variety of backgrounds all around the world. Opportunity calls, training calls, and more—all through teleconferencing. It's like a hotel meeting room on the phone! Awesome!

Network Marketing companies and independent distributors have become Masters of teleconferencing. They use this technology to prospect, train, brainstorm and plan their strategies.

How about the way our industry is using voice mail?

Network Marketers broadcast new product information, meeting schedules, events and promotions, motivational messages, training tips, daily assignments to huge distributor groups—all with the push of a voice mail button.

This menu-driven telephone technology lets callers: press 1 to learn all about these wonderful new products; press 2 to hear from successful distributors sharing their stories; press 3 for the next regional meeting in your area; press 4 for newsletter information; press 5 to order prospecting and training tools from the company catalog; press 6 for product ordering information; or press 0 for an operator now.

It's phenomenal!

What Else?

Fax-on-demand and fax-forwarding technology. By calling a central number, you can immediately receive, send or even broadcast promotional literature to or from any other fax machine anywhere in the world! Everything from a product information brochure to a distributor application to an announcement of a new promotion to a complete prospecting package—all with the push of a button or two!

Cellular telephones. I'll bet that more Network Marketers have phones in their cars and briefcases than Hollywood stars, or even Hollywood lawyers!

Network Marketers have pioneered the most efficient and effective business use of **three-way calling** for prospecting and sponsoring.

Satellite TV broadcasts. No, I'm not kidding. Believe it or not, there are a number of companies and distributor groups who are sending out their own opportunity meetings and training broadcasts via satellite.

How do I know that?

Because as I write this very sentence, I'm on a plane returning home from Dallas, Texas, after shooting a two-hour satellite training show for one of the fastest-growing Network Marketers in the world today.

Jeff's company broadcasts a weekly opportunity show via satellite, so he decided to pioneer his own weekly training and opportunity shows. Over 3,000 of his people already own satellite dishes and more than eighty are being added every day.

He broadcasts his shows after football games, special company broadcasts, or on the weekends when people get together with friends. The people in his network are inviting friends, associates and prospects over for barbecues, football and... "Oh, by the way, how would you like to see what our company is up to these days?" Powerful stuff: technology and Network Marketers at their best!

See, one thing is true about technology: at first, it's usually cost-prohibitive; reserved for a privileged and wealthy few. But sooner or later, the cost of new technology comes tumbling down. And when it does, especially after it has proven its value—everybody jumps in.

Remember what happened to the cost of videotape players? Digital watches? Calculators? And now computers? With more powerful computers at continually lower costs, we'll soon experience the biggest change in our lives—*the biggest change of all time!*

Network Marketing Enters The Computer Age

There is a revolution that's about to take place and it's going to change the way the world shops.

As our time becomes more precious, we create a greater need for convenience. One-stop shopping, in-

home shopping, home delivery, and advanced com-
puter-assisted technologies will dramatically impact
the way the world buys and sells. America—the
greatest consumer nation in the world—will witness
this change first. In fact, if you look, it's already begun.

Two of the biggest and fastest-growing marketing
segments in the American economy today are mail-
order catalogs and in-home shopping via cable TV.
(In my most recent visit to the United Kingdom, I witnessed the introduction of Great Britain's first home-
shopping network.) Exciting things are beginning to
mold our future.

Here's what futurist Faith Popcorn—who has had
an uncanny ability over the past two decades to accurately predict the trends that shape our future—says
in her latest book, *The Popcorn Report:*

> The home cocoon will be the site of the future
> shopping center. All members of the family will be
> able to shop from one location. Instead of going to
> the store, the store will come to us, no matter how
> unusual the product or how frequently needed. On
> our [computer and TV] screens, we'll be able to
> hear about the latest new products or styles, or or-
> der up our old favorites.

> Like the corporation, the shopping experience as
> we know it has grown cumbersome, inefficient, a
> violation of the trends. The big department stores
> are discovering that it's no longer possible to be all
> things to all customers. The shopping center is be-
> coming a dinosaur in the grand scheme of things.

> Today's mail-order catalogs and sale flyers (piled
> up in the house somewhere waiting to be thumbed

through and discarded) are obsolete—too much wasted paper, plus the post office is too inefficient, postage too expensive, to keep sending them through the mail.

The means of distribution will be the next consumer-oriented revolution. Direct shopping from the producer to you—bypassing the retailer altogether, no middlemen, no stops along the way.

Home delivery will become, not an extra service, but a way of life. One truck delivering to a hundred customers will be a much more efficient use of resources than a hundred customers driving to stores. There will be holding tanks in your house for milk, soda, mineral water (all refrigerated), and bins for laundry soap and dog kibble, for example, all delivered like home heating oil.*

In her book, Ms. Popcorn goes on to describe the shopping experience of the future. With the exception of very local or personal specialty shops and huge "emporiums where shopping becomes theater" (much like today's malls and theme parks), she describes three new offspring of buying and selling technology: "AdverNews"—advertising on your home computer screen, customized by you, according to your and your family's interests; "ScreenMail," where we'll shop, pay bills, receive and send information electronically; and "InfoBuying," where you'll bring up on your in-home computer or TV screen all of the information you need to make buying decisions and place an order for a new car, VCR, and the like.

All of this via computer, right in the comfort and

---

* Faith Popcorn, *The Popcorn Report* (Bantam Doubleday Dell Publishing Group, Inc., 1991), 164-5.

convenience of our own homes. Just what the Network Marketer of tomorrow ordered.

Too "far out" for you?

Well, just take a look at the extraordinary success of cable TV's home shopping channels and TV's living-catalog programs. And, friends, that's just round one.

It's been said that tomorrow's illiterates will be those people who can't operate a computer.

Believe me, I'm not John Mega Hertz, the Bits and Bytes man. I still write my books longhand! What I know about computers could fit in a flea's navel and still have room for two sesame seeds and a laser printer!

But I do know that computers are the wave of the future. Experts are predicting that by the year 2000, the developed world will be connected by a network of in-home computers. And if Network Marketing is also the wave of the future—as I'm convinced it is—the two had better start doing some serious courting, because there's a marriage that's about to happen real soon!

History Repeats Itself

Thirty years ago, a new way of doing business emerged called *franchising*, and the concept then seemed as alien as a world connected by personal computers is for some people today.

Back then, people called franchising a scam and a pyramid scheme. (Does this sound familiar?) At the time, the U.S. Congress fell just eleven votes short of completely outlawing franchising! It's true! No

McDonalds, Burger King, ServiceMaster, Century 21... none of them!

Yet today, franchising is a $765 billion dollar industry—yes, I said *billion*—responsible for thirty-five percent of all the goods and services consumers buy in America.

People resist change, and a computer in every home seems like a major change for most people. But the truth is that computers are the wave of the future.

I can see the day when all Network Marketing companies will be connected to each of their key distributors via the home computer. Distributors will electronically receive product information and genealogies, send and receive distributor applications, place orders, even get commission checks electronically transferred on their personal computers.

Here are some other examples of computer technology in action:

The words you're reading right this moment were once zipped around the country as little pieces of digitized on/off electronic impulses. That's right, dictated over the telephone, entered into the computer, modemed here and back to there—covering thousands of miles in just a few minutes. Then neatly put into a computer layout and design program, and finally—*plop*—out comes a book.

CD-ROM technology is already in wide use, and prices are plunging. Now an entire encyclopedia can be put on a CD and fed into a personal computer. How would you like to learn *anything* from the top five experts on any subject in the world? And learn it at your own pace, whenever you wanted, with pictures, words and sounds that appeared according to your questions and answers? You can, right now, with computers.

And remember, I don't know much about computers at all; yet, here I am, right smack in the middle of the future of it all.

The Master Prospectors of tomorrow will be on-line, plugged-in, turned-on and connected to each other through their computer networks. You know, nothing networks like a bunch of computers, and no group of people network like Network Marketers. We were made for each other!

With so many technological choices out there, it's never been more important to plan and investigate all of your options. This Action Step will get you started on the road to your future—today!

MY ACTION STEPS

to Mastery of Secret #12:

Master Prospectors live in the future—today!

1) What forms of technology will I investigate and learn more about using? New, more productive ways that I can build my business of the future— today.

_____

_____

_____

_____

_____

_____

_____

_____

_____

_____

_____

_____

Master Prospectors know how to hit their targets

As I've said earlier, Network Marketers are paid to advertise: If we don't advertise, we don't get paid! There are a number of ways to advertise; some cost more money than time, and others cost more time than money. This secret is about getting the most out of all your advertising money *and* time!

My friend Robert Butwin, the MLMIA's Distributor of the Year for two years in a row, lost nearly $100,000 in his first few years in this business—most of it, he admits, due to ineffective advertising. Robert calls it the most expensive lesson of his life. Obviously, he learned his lesson well.

I don't want you to pay that high of a price. It's not necessary when you can learn a few things from the Masters.

Advertising: A Specialist Game

Do you remember the Greek myth about Prometheus? He stole fire from the gods on Mt. Olympus to give to humankind, and as punishment, Zeus chained him to a rock where an eagle tore at his liver. Well, until you learn where, when and how to compete against the "big boys" or "gods" with your advertising dollars, don't do it! You might end up like Prometheus.

Don't think that I'm saying that you shouldn't advertise at all. I *am* saying this: Expensive advertising is a specialty game, and you need to be a specialist to play it well.

The mistake most new distributors make in advertising is approaching it like they're already one of the "gods." Yet most of them don't have the experience or financial resources to do so. Most Master Prospectors recommend so-called "guerilla," or "grass-roots" advertising to their new distributors. It's a great way for their new people to get their feet wet and learn some valuable rules of the advertising game.

Small Can Be Beautiful

When new distributors begin to consider advertising for their Network Marketing businesses, most of them turn to where they've already seen ads. They see these big, quarter- to full-page display ads in industry publications, or they see business opportunity ads in national publications and think they need to do the same to compete.

Here's the first rule of the specialty game: *Don't compete directly with advertisers who are much bigger than you are—unless you can afford to.*

Why this rule? Because advertising, at that level, is about *consistency* and *dominance*.

Most ads will not draw well until people see them enough times that it moves them into action—some analysts say at least fifteen times. In order to be seen, your ad must appear *consistently* enough and be big enough to *dominate* the medium—or at least dominate the page where it appears.

The "Small Is Beautiful" strategy is ideal for new distributors wanting to get into the advertising game. The idea is to hit your prospects where the "big boys" aren't.

Ads Targeted To People You Know

Big advertisers you don't want to compete with are not usually in your warm market—your own circle of influence. Here's where you've got a sizeable advantage over the "big boys." So advertise to people who you already know or know about via flyers, newsletters, postcards, three-step mailings, and the like.

"But *that's* not advertising!" you say.

It most certainly is!

Advertising at its very best is simply saying the right things to the right people. A button that says, "Lose weight now. Ask me how!" is sure saying the right thing to a person concerned about weight loss.

How about a flyer sent to all of the women you know with a headline that says, "At last, a product that erases laugh lines with a price that makes you smile."

Or how about a small poster that begins, "Bottled

water for only 4¢ a gallon" posted above the drinking fountain at your health club?

These are all examples of simple, warm-market ads which have been used successfully by hundreds of Networkers over the years. The cost of the time and money you spend to print and send them out is small and the return of quality leads can be large. You'll also gain valuable marketing experience— you'll find out what works and doesn't work with minimal financial risk.

Advertise Where They Aren't

Just think for a moment about where you've seen ads for Network Marketing products and opportunities. Now think about where you *haven't* seen them.

Local ads in smaller-circulation newspapers—or what we call "penny-savers" in the U.S.—is one place where the "big boys" aren't.

One of the places to advertise that I recommend most is in the "personals" of a local newspaper's classified section. Did you know that the personals are read five times more frequently than the rest of the classifieds?

Here's an ad that had great success when used in a local paper's "personals":

Lost Your Phone Number!
Would the family that wanted a good second income opportunity please call John at 555-1234.

This is an inexpensive ad that would get between five and ten calls a week. Doesn't sound like a lot of leads, you say? Stop and think for a moment about who called. Were these the kind of people you'd have to spend a lot of time with trying to figure out if they wanted to earn additional income? And were these prospects calling all the other business opportunity ads in the paper—all of your competitors' ads? Highly unlikely!

Wouldn't it be a great start to have five to ten interested, qualified people calling *you* every week, asking to hear about your income-earning opportunity? How would you like to have a minimum of 250 people call you each year wanting to know more about what you had to offer?

Here's another ad a Master Prospector friend of mine ran in the personals of her local paper that did wonderfully. It was fun and inexpensive for her to do.

Who's Mary?
She's an expert at finding easy and fun ways to make a second income for people. Call her today at...

True, not a truckload of people responded, but enough qualified, interested people called to keep Mary busy. Several of them entered the business and did well enough to provide Mary with over a 2,000% return on that one ad campaign alone!

On Target

Remember what I said about saying the right things to the right people?

The real secret to effective ads that build your Network Marketing business is targeting the people you want to advertise to. In other words, who do you want to respond to your ads? Everyone and anyone? Do you really have the time to sort through everyone and anyone? Or would you want your ad to do a big chunk of the sorting for you?

The most common advertising mistake is when people go for big numbers and forget that the *quality* of those numbers is at least as important. The ads above may not burn up the telephone with hundreds of leads, but those who do call are already pre-qualified to a certain degree—before you even have to say a word. You may also find that a far higher percentage of these people will come into your business and flourish than those who commonly respond to run-of-the-mill opportunity ads.

So make a list of the different types of people you know. Separate them into the smallest categories you can think of: retirees, schoolteachers, executives, golfers, mothers who use baby-sitters, and so forth. Then experiment with different headlines and offers that would appeal to these specific groups of people. Also, think of the best locations or publications to place your ads. You're *targeting* those categories of people.

> **Interested In Earning Part-Time Retirement Income?**
> Now that you have the time, how about the money to enjoy it?

> **Attention Golfers: Earn Extra Income On The Back Nine**
> Get paid to play—and write off your golf clubs, too.

> **For Busy Executives**
> Would you like to have an income-generating asset equal to $150,000 in growth stock dividends? Low risk, with tax-advantages?

I can't vouch for the success of any of the above ads. I just made them up to get you thinking of ways to target specific kinds of people with your products, service or opportunity.

My point is to go after narrow groups with your advertising efforts. There's less competition and a far greater chance of reaching interested, enthusiastic people than using a broad-based, shotgun approach. And it's a lot cheaper too.

The key is to be different.

Just Had A Thought

I'm sitting here under the shade of a majestic old tree looking across the bay at the picturesque city of Sydney, Australia. This is my first trip to this beautiful part of the world.

I've got a day off during a three-week seminar tour throughout Australia and New Zealand, so I chose a peaceful place to relax and work on my book. A thought just crossed my mind that deserves some space here.

I just pictured a host of Network Marketing publishers—who count on distributor advertising dollars for their publications—getting a bit upset over the previous section.

I don't want to alienate these industry leaders. They provide a great service to the industry. My goal here is to simply offer you some alternatives.

A greater number of advertising choices will increase your chances for success—especially if you can try them without risking a large percentage of your start-up capital. By starting small at first, you can expand your experience in advertising as well as your advertising budget! When you can make advertising work for you at the grass-roots level, you're well on your way to playing and winning at the "Specialty Game."

It's kind of like playing baseball in the minor

leagues to hone your skills and build your self-confidence before you break into the major leagues.

Many excellent athletes with a lot of potential have been pressured to play with the "big boys" before they were ready. If they didn't get off to a fast start—hit a couple of home runs or make a crowd-pleasing catch—we never heard from them again.

Well, many excellent new distributors with a lot of potential tried to play with the "big boys" of advertising before they were ready, also. The result was virtually the same—they were never heard from again.

Master Prospectors, like the good managers they are, look at their new recruits and see a lot of potential. Potential that usually needs to be coached and nurtured.

Teaching their new recruits the grass-roots fundamentals of advertising and providing them the "field of opportunity" to hone their skills and develop self-confidence means a larger number of seasoned players in their network that are getting ready to play in the big leagues.

If Network Marketing publishers saw an increase in the number of experienced advertisers who know the value of long-running ads (instead of an irregular supply of inexperienced "I'll try it a couple of times" advertisers) then maybe they won't look down on what I'm trying to teach you. I hope so, anyway!

Everybody Loves A Crowd (Of Prospects)

Many companies do not want their distributors to exhibit their products at flea markets and swap meets. There's a kind of "low class" stigma attached to these gatherings, and many companies don't want to encourage that kind of image. Trade shows, however, are another matter.

Some trade shows can be expensive propositions. Of course, there are ways to team up with other distributors and share the cost of booth space and expenses. This strategy may make it possible for beginning distributors to attend some of the bigger trade shows. There are some small, local trade shows, and local chapters of national organizations that have shows, too. These can be far less expensive to participate in.

Trade shows are a great way to meet lots of people. It's kind of like targeting a big crowd of prospects in one place at one time.

Target your trade shows the same way you'd target your ads. Be different. Don't try to compete with the "big boys." Don't take your skin-care products to a health and beauty aids show and sit there in a booth next to Revlon with their fifteen Vogue models and $250,000 product display.

Play the grass-roots game here, too. You can do local health and lifestyles shows, fitness expos, and local business opportunity conferences. This is a great way to get your feet wet and hone your skills!

Let's go back to the flea markets and the swap meets for a moment.

As I said, most companies don't want their products displayed for sale at these shows. But a lot of people frequent these places. So what if you take a different approach? Here's what a couple of savvy Master Prospectors have done with great success.

Approach #1: Market Research

If you have a product that can be sampled, you can create a questionnaire. Have people simply try the product, taste it, put some on—whatever demonstration works best—and then have them fill out a simple form where they can say what they thought about it.

Design the form to look official with boxes that they can check off. Ask a variety of "marketing questions," and have a place at the bottom for their name, address and phone number. You might also want to create a coupon that gives them a discount on purchasing the product they sampled and liked.

Afterwards, simply follow-up with them. Remember that following-up with the prospects you generate is the key to every form of advertising you try. If you don't have a good, easy-to-use follow-up system yet, get one!

Approach #2: Career Survey

Get a team of your associates together and give this a try. Create a survey that helps people identify what they like and don't like about their current work situation. Have questions they can answer that trigger the importance of things like creativity, freedom, flexible hours, no commuting, being their own boss, residual income, and so on.

Interact with them as they answer the career survey, focusing your attention on building rapport with them. Have fun with it! You'll find most people very willing to open up to you and share both their likes and dislikes in what they do. (You'll find sample questions for a "Career Survey" at the end of this secret. Don't think you have to use *only* these questions. Use them to trigger your own ideas and to get you headed in the right direction.)

If, upon completing the career survey, the prospect seems to be an ideal candidate for the business, you can give them some information that explains the concept of Network Marketing. There are a number of generic brochures you can use, or you can make up your own. Some prospects would be open to giving you a $10 to $20 refundable deposit for a generic book and video that educates them about what Network Marketing is—and what it is not.

Again, follow-up is the key. So get their name, address and phone number, and get back to them when you said you would.

Making A Name For Yourself

Perhaps the hardest aspect of prospecting is making people aware of what you have to offer. If you are so inclined and are bold enough, there are some promotional avenues you can pursue that can get the "awareness" job done. They come under the heading of *promotions* or *public relations (PR)*.

The more you learn about Network Marketing, the more you become an expert in a unique field—a field that the vast majority of men and women still know very little about. Do you know enough to be able to talk with various groups and associations in your community about Network Marketing? It may be easier than you think, and it's a great way to build awareness about you and your industry.

A number of Master Prospectors I know have given talks to local Rotary and Kiwanis clubs, business associations, and networking groups. They keep their talks "generic" and don't "present" their specific opportunity when they speak. What often happens is that people come up to them afterwards wanting to know how they can learn more about Network Marketing. Sometimes they ask about how one gets involved in the business.

Fill your talk with solid truth about our industry. Learn as much as you can and put together a twenty- or thirty-minute presentation.

Associations, clubs, and even the business or marketing departments at community high schools and colleges are eager to have speakers on new topics. And believe me, you don't have to be a seasoned, polished, professional speaker to get a standing ovation. Preparation and practice is the key.

Also, local media such as newspapers and radio stations are often looking for people to talk about newsworthy subjects. If you're involved in an interview, be prepared to answer some of the misunderstandings that exist about our business. By telling the truth and not being defensive, you'll go a long way with your audience.

If you've got products that lend themselves to charity donations or support of humanitarian causes, work with your company or upline sponsors and find ways to donate these items to those less fortunate. Examples of this are: nutritional products for homeless shelters; pet products for local animal-cruelty groups; skin-care or personal-care products for use by the elderly in nursing homes; nutritional snacks for daycare centers, and so on. Take a camera along and maybe even a local reporter to get an article written about your good works. It's a big benefit for Network Marketing's public image and an even bigger benefit for you.

Imagine making a presentation to a prospect who says, "I know you. You're the gal who helps those kids at the hospital..." Or, "Yeah, I've seen you on TV, taking care of those dogs down at the animal shelter."

Nice work! And do you know why so few people get this kind of positive publicity? Because they don't try. That's all. It's a lot easier than you may think.

Building An International Business

Colin is a new friend of mine in Australia; he's a great guy, and well on his way to becoming a Master Prospector. The Network Marketing company he is with will soon be expanding into other countries such as Malaysia and the Philippines, and Colin's dream is to grow his business internationally.

He's running ads in his local Australian papers and targeting prospects who have contacts in Malaysia or the Philippines. Prospects that would be interested in helping an explosive, fast-growing Australian company open up these exciting new markets.

When prospects respond (usually only one or two per week), he sits down with them and explains his entire opportunity.

If the prospect is interested, he helps them focus on who they know locally (in Australia) so they can get things started while they're waiting for the other countries to open up.

I am confident that by the time Colin's company is ready to do business in these other countries, he'll have four or five well-trained, fired-up distributors with excellent foreign contacts. He can travel with them to Malaysia and the Philippines and begin building the international business of his (and their) dreams.

This powerful strategy is not only limited to international expansion. You can use a similar plan to open up other cities or regions of your country—areas where you'd like to grow your business.

In fact, here's a great rule of thumb if you're thinking of expanding your business outside of your local area: *plan before you act!* And base your planning on this rule: *Think globally but act locally!*

Now this is not to say you should never travel to expand your business—eventually that will become necessary and it's one of the great benefits of being a global networker. Just make sure you're doing everything you can locally before you pack your bags.

You'll be amazed at how many business-building strategies you can come up with that will allow you to act locally, yet build globally. And the more productive you are locally, the more duplicatable you become, and the more "bang" you get for your business "buck"!

It's Everywhere

The whole point of advertising in Network Marketing is to not limit your thinking to doing it just one way— the business opportunity section. Master Prospectors see advertising opportunities everywhere, because that's just where they are—*they're everywhere!*

And remember: Master Prospectors are into targeting their advertising and hitting their targets.

Why? Because hitting the "bull's eye" my friend, is the name of the game!

———————————

How would you like to make your advertising efforts a hit? Good! Use the Action Steps below to set your sights on a few targets.

MY ACTION STEPS

to Mastery of Secret #13:

Master Prospectors know how to hit their targets

1) What kind of advertising campaign would I like to create within the next ninety days to promote my business?

_____

_____

_____

_____

_____

_____

_____

_____

2) I want to target my message to the following
    groups of people:

_____

_____

_____

_____

_____

_____

_____

_____

3) Where would I like to advertise?

_____

_____

_____

_____

_____

_____

_____

_____

_____

4) How would I like to advertise?

_____

_____

_____

_____

_____

_____

_____

_____

_____

5) How much am I willing to invest each month for the next three months into my advertising budget?

Month One: $_____

Month Two: $_____

Month Three: $_____

Sample Career Survey

1. Do you like your work? ....□ □
2. Do you like who you work for? ....□ □
3. Are you earning what you're worth? ....□ □
4. Does your job offer good chances for advancement? ......□ □
5. Does your career challenge you? ....□ □
6. Do you have variety in your career? ....□ □
7. Do you want to be doing you're present job when
    you're 60? ....□ □
8. Is your income sufficient to satisfy your needs? ....□ □
9. Do you get enough time off to do all the things
    you want? ....□ □
10. Are you now working at only one job? ....□ □

If you answered "no" to two questions or less, your career is in good shape. If you answered "no" to three or four questions, you might consider another occupation. If you answered "no" to five or more questions, you definitely need to look for another line of work!

1. Do you like teaching and talking with people? ....□ □
2. Do you like sharing things you're excited about
    with others? ....□ □
3. Would you like more money *and* more tax deductions? ..□ □
4. Would you like an exciting career that makes
    others happy? ....□ □
5. Do you like challenge and variety in your career? ....□ □
6. Would you like a career with unlimited income
    potential? ....□ □
7. Does being your own boss and having more free
    time sound interesting to you? ....□ □
8. Would you like more people to respect and admire you? □ □
9. Would you like to travel and deduct the expenses
    from your taxes? ....□ □
10. Would you be willing to work twenty hours a week for
    the next twelve months? ....□ □

If you answered "yes" to the first nine questions, we need to set an appointment at your earliest convenience. If you answered "yes" to all ten questions, we need to sit down and talk! Please fill in the information below and I'll get in touch with you within 48 hours.

[Leave space for their name, address, phone and best time to call, along with your address and phone number]

Secret #14

Master Prospectors
know what and how to ask

Does this scene sound familiar?

Your customer: "Well, I'm really looking forward to trying these products—when can I start?"

You: "I have the products with me, so you can get started on them immediately. I know you're going to love them! Oh, one last thing—who else do you know that might be interested?"

Your customer (looking at the ceiling, thinking and pausing): "Gosh, I can't think of anyone off-hand.... But if I do, I'll be sure to let you know."

And they don't call you with the names of other people, do they? Even though they're enthusiastic about your product (and maybe also your business opportunity) and they know and like you well enough to genuinely want to help you, they don't.

Why? One main reason: You haven't asked in the right way.

This secret is about asking for help from people you know in such a way that you consistently get lots of names of others who are very likely to be interested in your product and/or your opportunity.

It's a strategy we call The Master Prospector's referral process, a simple step-by-step method for obtaining great referrals. (By the way, the person from whom you obtain names is called your "referral source," and the person he or she refers you to is the "referral.") So let's begin!

Why Building Your Business Through Referrals Is More Fun

First of all, it's much easier to approach someone who is a "friend of a friend."

Imagine starting out by saying, "Hi, Laura, it's Suzanne Smith calling. I was talking to Randy Owens the other day and he suggested I give you a call because...." Hopefully, Laura will be much more open to what you have to say right from the outset—especially if Randy is someone she particularly likes and respects.

It's a reality of your Network Marketing business that you'll need to talk to a lot of people. Let's say you have a goal of talking to ten new people every week. Wouldn't you like to use less energy to find and talk to these ten? Well, the process is much easier if you're approaching people with whom you have at least an indirect connection. It's a lot tougher to get a complete stranger to give you an hour of their time. Imagine how much *less* time and effort it would take talking to people with whom you have a common friend!

The Problem With Asking For Referrals

If it's easier to approach referrals and it takes less time, why don't we ask for referrals more often?

Maybe we forget. That's easy enough to do, especially when we're excited about starting with a new customer. Or maybe we have a resistance to asking for help. Or maybe it's because, deep down, we realize that if the tables were turned, *we wouldn't feel comfortable giving out the names of our own friends!*

Let's look more closely at this "discomfort factor." There are three main reasons why people feel uncomfortable about giving referrals.

First, they may not be comfortable with your product or service (or with Network Marketing in general).

Second, they may be wary of what you're going to say to their contacts, and they may not want to be quoted as giving a recommendation or endorsement.

And third, your referral source doesn't want his or her contacts to be annoyed by your approach and, in turn, annoyed at him for giving you their names.

Let's look at each of these "discomfort factors" in turn. Learning how to address these is the beginning of the referral process.

Discomfort Factor #1: Uneasiness With Product Or Network Marketing In General

You can address this one by carefully planning in advance who you will ask for referrals.

Rule Number One: Only ask people with whom you've "earned the right" to ask. If you barely know

someone, you may feel uncomfortable asking for referrals—that's a signal that you haven't yet earned
the right.

There are two categories of people from whom
you automatically have the right to ask for referrals.

The first category is small and includes your clos-
est family and friends. You have earned the right
with them, because they obviously care about you
and your success.

The second (and much bigger) category of good
candidates to ask for referrals is your customers!
Once they are happy users of your product or service, they are perfect candidates for obtaining referrals. One caution: try to avoid asking them until they
are enjoying and are delighted with your product.
This is when their enthusiasm for sharing the benefits will be the highest and you will have truly
earned the right to ask.

Rule Number Two: Educate your referral sources
about your business.

Whether your referral source is a family member,
neighbor or happy customer, you will usually need to
educate them (at least a little) about your Network
Marketing business before they will feel open to giving you referrals.

Some people can still feel cautious about "those
multi-level things," because they haven't been prop-
erly educated about it. For those with open minds, invest the time to share with them why Network Marketing is a modern, viable and professional method of
distribution.

Another caution: in our enthusiasm for this great industry, there is often a big temptation to dump a load of information on our referral source to justify why we are in this business. Keep it short, matter-of-fact and linked to one or two "success stories." Concise, calm conviction is the most persuasive style. Maybe share with them a book or video on the subject of Network Marketing—the more generic the content, the better!

Discomfort Factor #2: What You Are Going To Say To The Referrals

When asked for referrals, people may feel uncomfortable giving you names, because they think you will be telling the referral that they endorsed or recommended the product or business opportunity.

This discomfort stems from their desire to protect their reputation in case the referral doesn't like what you present. A difference of opinion could mean that the referral might lose respect or confidence in the person who referred them. No one wants this to happen, especially you.

So, the way to address this is to come right out and tell your referral source what you will be saying to the referral. Reassure them that you won't be saying that they recommended or endorsed your product.

You should develop a standard script that you can quote to your referral source. Make the wording your own—the point is to be able to quote it to the referral source.

Focus on giving information and ideas, not selling.

Discomfort Factor #3:
"Don't Bother My Friends"

Again the real fear here is that the referral source might jeopardize a valued relationship with the referral if you annoy him when you call.

The best way to address this fear is to have the referral source become so enthusiastic about the potential benefits to the referral that he genuinely wants you to call. If he is a happy customer, he will already know the benefits of the product. Then the question is simply: "Is there a good possibility that your referral could also be interested in this product?"

In order to answer this question, you will need to have done some homework. You must be able to describe (in some detail) the kinds of people that are your best and happiest customers. People that will be most open—and even excited—to hear about the product or opportunity. This description is what we call "Your Ideal Referral Profile."

The Ideal Prospect

On a sheet of paper, write down the characteristics of your most satisfied customers or distributors. What products do they buy? Male or female? Age range? Where located geographically? How much do they earn? Occupation? Why do they buy your products? Who do they know? How loyal are they? Personality traits? Values? Interests? Ability to pay? Hobbies or recreational activities?

One particular question should always be put on your list: Does the referral know, like and respect the referral source? If they are merely acquaintances or there isn't respect between them, then using the referral source's name has minimal value.

Here's an example of an Ideal Referral Profile (for a nutritional product):

- Health conscious, exercises regularly
- Has mentioned lack of energy
- Is "on the go" a lot
- Age 25 to 50
- Buys vitamins or other supplements (willing to invest in health)
- Interested in learning better ways to take care of themselves.

Your actual list can and should be longer, and when you share it with your referral source, you will need to point out that just two or three of these characteristics are enough for that person to be a potentially good candidate.

Using this Ideal Referral Profile will help immensely in assisting your referral source to think about the right kinds of people for you to approach and, in turn, show him that these people are very likely to be interested.

Let's recap the key points we've learned here for the referral process:

1. List referral sources with whom you have earned the right to ask (remember the two main categories).

2. Call referral sources and ask if they would be willing to help you. If so, make an appointment. (Prepare your phone script in advance.)

3. Arrive on time for the appointment, remind the referral source of their willingness to help, set a time limit for the meeting and explain your objec-

tive—getting six or seven referrals. (Again, prepare a script ahead of time!)

4. *Briefly* educate your referral source about the product and business opportunity: what it is, why you love it, how's it's different, and a short success story or two.

5. Tell your referral source what you will say when calling referrals.

6. Ensure there is a "true fit"—use your Ideal Referral Profile.

7. Ask: "Who comes to mind first?"

8. If they get stuck after one or two names, suggest they use their personal directory, business card file, Christmas card list or computer directory.

9. List the names first, then go back and ask for particulars to ensure they fit at least part of the Ideal Referral Profile.

10. Follow-up: Call your referral source about the positive results you got with their referrals—and ask for more!

Let's Try It Again

Remember the conversation we had earlier? Let's take a look at the difference now.

Your customer: "Well, I'm amazed at how great I feel and all the energy I have! Does everyone get the same quick results?"

You: "Yes, it's a very consistent product if people give it a chance. I'm pleased you're so pleased! Randy, remember when we talked on the phone, you said you knew some other people you cared about? People you'd love to see feel as good as you?"

Your customer: "Sure..."

You: "Well, I thought it would be great if we could come up with six or seven names. And by the way, I always want to make sure that when I ask my satisfied customers for referrals that they're completely comfortable about me talking to their friends. So, let me refresh your memory a little about how I'll approach them.

"After I introduce myself, here's the kind of thing I'll probably say: 'Hi, Susan, I was talking with Randy Owens the other day and he suggested I give you a call. I understand you know Randy from the Little League parents group? Well, Randy said you were very keen and serious about your health. I have some ideas to share with you that have made a tremendous difference with Randy. That's why he gave me your name and number...' And then I would go on to ask when we could get together."

Your customer: "OK, that's fine."

You: "By the way, Randy, here's the type of person who can benefit the most from our products (share Ideal Referral Profile). I don't expect you to know anyone with all of these characteristics, but if there are people you know who have two or three of them, I'm sure those people would benefit tremendously. Who comes to your mind first?"

(Be prepared to wait in silence for awhile and be patient while they think. Anything you say now will only distract them.)

Your customer: "Well, there's Gail Sheineman next door... and Larry Bowers, I guess."

You: "Great.... You know, some people find it helpful to use their personal telephone directory...."

Your customer: "Oh, that's a good idea.... Now, let me see here. Oh, there's Susan Abbott.... and Luke Brown.... Nancy Chen.... Vince Dundee... and...."

Quite a difference, yes? When you form the habit of using this process with all your good customers, you will further develop your relationship with them and with their friends—plus widen and deepen your own circle of friendships in the process.

Once you master this secret, you may never have to make another "cold call" again!

We Want Your Input!

Let us know what you think of this secret and whether you'd like to learn more on the art of getting quality referrals for your products and business opportunity.

My friend and business associate Christine Elliot helped me put this secret together for you. She's a true Master in the referral process and has an incredible amount of information and proven techniques on the subject.

If you'd like, we can put together a specialty book *just about referrals* that will empower you and your business. Let us know if you'd like us to tackle the project!

This is a very powerful secret, and using it can make a huge difference in your business in a very short period of time. You'll begin to reap the benefits as soon as you start completing the questions below.

MY ACTION STEPS
to Mastery of Secret #14:

Master Prospectors
know what and how to ask

1) What is the "Ideal Customer Referral Profile" for my product?

_____

_____

_____

_____

_____

_____

_____

_____

_____

_____

_____

2) What is the "Ideal Business Referral Profile" for my opportunity?

_____

_____

_____

_____

_____

_____

_____

_____

3) How will I ask my referral sources for referrals? What will I say?

_____

_____

_____

_____

_____

_____

_____

_____

_____

_____

_____

Secret #15

Master Prospectors know that something for nothing is usually good for nothing

----

*W*hat's your opinion—do you believe in something for nothing? Life's experiences tell us that there's usually a promise made or a price to be paid. Here's an example you might relate to.

Half-Full Or Half-Empty?

In the early 1990s, our world experienced interesting and challenging economic times. Some people even believed we were on the verge of a world depression. In some areas of many countries, thousands of men and women lost their jobs, industries had to tighten their belts, and some companies and industries disappeared altogether.

Yet there were other areas within those same countries which experienced a "boom." Many industries prospered and thrived, creating many new jobs and opportunities.

Is the glass half-full or half-empty? Or as one comedian said, "Is the glass just too damn big?"

I'm not an economist, but I do know that the so-called "global recession" was bad news for some people and great news for others. I think it's pretty simple. If, in your opinion, we were in the midst of a recession and experiencing tough times, then that was probably true for you. On the other hand, if you saw the changing economic landscape as a time of tremendous opportunity, then that's what you experienced.

Garbage In, Garbage Out

We all have our opinions and most of us love to share them. Although some are positive and supportive, most people's opinions are negative and destructive.

To me, this "input" of other people's opinions (either positive or negative) is much like programming a computer. And, I'm sure you've heard the saying, "Garbage in, garbage out."

Imagine, if you will, that our brains are like the "hardware" of a computer—the monitor, hard drive, keyboard—all of the mechanical stuff that makes it a computer system. Since we all have a brain—virtually the same brain—we all have virtually the same computer system.

What makes people think and function differently is their "software." The software we choose for our computer (which determines how positively or negatively our brain operates) is made up of all of the opinions that we buy into. If we buy into negative (re- cession and hard time) software, then that's how we think and live—and we walk around feeling sorry for ourselves. If we invest in positive (new opportunities through change) and supportive software, then we perceive things in a positive light. We act accordingly and create success in our lives.

In my opinion, all the negative software that people buy into—the cascade of unsupportive opin- ions that we hear from others—is *dysfunctional soft- ware*. It's garbage. It doesn't serve us, so it doesn't work!

So, why do you think so many people buy this dys- functional software for their computers?

Because it's free! A perfect example of how some- thing for nothing is good for nothing.

It doesn't cost anything to get this dysfunctional software—and it's all around us. Turn on the TV— you'll see and hear dysfunctional software that doesn't support your success. Pick up the newspaper and you'll read some more dysfunctional software.

And if by chance you're not getting enough of it, have a chat with your neighbors. More than likely, they'll be happy to give you some of their dysfunc- tional software—*at no charge.*

On the other hand, the good software—that which is positive and supports our success—takes more ef- fort to get. Not surprisingly, it also comes with a price tag!

Not only do you need to *hunt* for this good soft- ware, you have to *pay* for it with your money and your time. That's why most people don't have good "mental software"—they're not willing to pay for it. They would just as soon settle on something for nothing.

Now some people might argue, "Well, if something doesn't cost anything, how could it *not* be worth it?"

Well, how would you feel about using a software program that was given to you free, but you later found out that it had an outrageous cost that was hidden from you at first—and you'd been paying for it all along? Would you still want that "free" software program? Not likely.

You see, when it comes to software programs for your mental computer, there are two types of costs:

1) Out-of-pocket, and

2) Out-of-potential.

With out-of-pocket costs, you know exactly what you're getting. You know the price and you know if it's worth it at the time you buy it.

Out-of-potential costs are hidden (because they appear free), but when you eventually discover the costs, they are *outrageously outrageous*.

The Masters of Network Marketing avoid software that carries out-of-potential costs. They'd rather pay now—out of their pocket.

Why? Because in their minds (thanks to their good software), *their potential worth is far greater than their present worth*.

It's quite simple: Master Prospectors understand that out-of-potential costs (dysfunctional software programs) rob them of their future. *And there's noth-*

*ing that's worth the cost of your tomorrow, no matter
how easy and free it is to get today.*

Seek And Ye Shall Find

Master Prospectors are always seeking newer, more
powerful software no matter what the out-of-pocket
costs are. Why? Because they believe their computer
is worth it!

They reject the negative programming of
unsupportive opinions that are all around them and
focus on what works and supports them.

How do they do this? Good question. Here are
some examples:

Master Prospectors invest in themselves. They
are constantly "upgrading" their software with education and learning. They subscribe to publications
that improve their skills and attitude. They read
books and listen to tapes that increase their mastery
of *all* aspects of their Network Marketing business.
They attend workshops, seminars, company conventions, meetings and trainings. They are always ready
to learn something new that will empower their life
and work.

Master Prospectors invest in their people. They
invest time training their associates. They help their
new distributors sponsor others, both on the phone
and through live presentations. They constantly promote events that bring in professionals and other
sales leaders to train their people. They create lend-
ing libraries of books and tapes, so that the men and
women in their distributor networks always have the
latest versions of the best software.

Master Prospectors don't devalue their product or opportunity. They offer their products at full retail, because they know their products are worth it. They don't recommend that people get into the business just to be wholesale consumers. They see buying "wholesale" as a benefit and a privilege and they offer it that way. They also don't build people's networks for them. Stacking people under other people creates a sense of false achievement, and unearned advancement is something for nothing.

Master Prospectors see the true value and desirability of their products. They know that their opportunity is a wonderful gift. And they accept responsibility for the success of their associates by giving them training and support.

Master Prospectors place a high value on *value* because they know that something for nothing is usually good for nothing. Master Prospectors are *investors*. They invest their time, money, effort and energy into building their businesses, and they expect a return that's far greater than their investment. And Master Prospectors are always teaching their people to do the same!

I'll bet you're getting pretty good at doing these Action Steps by now. That's because you know they're worth it—and expecting something for doing nothing is not your style!

MY ACTION STEPS

to Mastery of Secret #15:

Master Prospectors know that something for nothing is usually good for nothing

1) What out-of-potential costs and dysfunctional software have I been buying into? Which negative people and what unsupportive environments have I been allowing to rob me of my future?

_____

_____

_____

_____

_____

_____

_____

_____

_____

_____

_____

_____

_____

_____

_____

2) What corrective measures can I take to avoid
    any future out-of-potential costs?

    _____

    _____

    _____

    _____

    _____

    _____

    _____

    _____

    _____

    _____

3) What amount of out-of-pocket investment am I
    willing to make each month for the next three
    months that will empower my belief system in
    myself and my future?

    Month #1: $ _____

    Month #2: $ _____

    Month #3: $ _____

4) What are the best ways that I can invest these
    amounts? (List approximate costs of each
    investment.)

Month #1

_____

_____

_____

_____

_____

_____

Month #2

_____

_____

_____

_____

_____

_____

Month #3

_____

_____

_____

_____

_____

_____

Secret #16

Master Prospectors study and model the Masters

---

*W*hat is the single fastest track you can take to become a Master Prospector?

It's simple: study the Masters of Prospecting.

As I've said before, I like to consider myself twice the student that I am the teacher. And what I've learned over the years about prospecting has come— as the ancients used to say—"at the feet of the Masters."

My friend Tom Schreiter, author of the hugely successful "Big Al" books, has always said that the key to building leaders in our business is to move in with your people for six months; teach them all you know; and then, when they are smarter, sharper, and better than you are, move on.

If you're committed to becoming a Master Prospector, simply reverse the procedure.

Modeling And Mirroring Revisited

Do you remember when we talked about building rapport in Secret #6? We discussed modeling and mirroring your prospect's speech patterns, posture, eye movements and breathing in order to create a sense of harmony with them.

Well, when you're in the company of Master Prospectors, do the same thing and take it one step further. Here's what I mean:

Apply all of the material you learned about building rapport to your study of the Masters of Prospecting. Focus first on the outside stuff: the way they look and act. Check out their posture, how they walk and talk, everything. Focus on the details and then mirror and model what you've observed.

Now, a warning: This is not "Send In The Clones." I'm not asking you to become a robot copy of another person—no matter how successful they are. I'm suggesting that the Master Prospectors that you're studying have learned many ways of being and behaving, all stemming from successful experiences. So why reinvent the wheel? Maybe some of that same behavior can work for you.

Take what they show you and try it on for size. The rule is simply this: if you like the shoe and it fits—wear it. And if it feels good to wear it—perhaps a certain way of speaking, a particular posture or behavior—then make it your very own. And if you can't find a way to "own it," then throw it out. But try it on first.

Check it out. See what it looks, sounds or feels like before you pass judgement.

One Master Prospector I studied was a great speaker. I watched him for hours as he led trainings, made presentations, and conducted one-on-one prospecting interviews. I marveled at how people responded to him and at the exceptional results he got. Whether he was in front of a group of people or speaking to just one person, he carried himself the same way. He always spoke quickly and with a tremendous amount of enthusiasm. He was a true pro and a great role model.

One day I asked him to give me a few pointers on how to be a better public speaker. He put his hand on my shoulder and said, "John, you're very good. One thing you can try to do is to speak faster. When you pause like you do, you lose some of your audience."

Well, I thought about that and decided to give it a try. The next few times I spoke to groups, I talked a lot faster. I whizzed through my presentations like Machine-Gun Kalench. Wow!

Here's what I found: some of it worked and some of it didn't.

You Gotta Be You

Many people have told me that my soft-spoken style encouraged them to listen more, and that they could really feel my sincerity. Well, almost no one told me that after I gave those "fast-forward" talks.

So I decided to go back to my natural soft-and-slow style, except for a couple of sections of my talk where

I wanted to show some real enthusiasm. In those parts, I put my mentor's speedier style to work.

The result? I started getting my best receptions ever.

Why? Because that's how most people perceive and know me when I'm *not* in front of the room. It's my natural, comfortable style to speak softly and deliberately.

Completely changing my style didn't work for me. It was incongruent with who I am most of the time. Yet by adjusting a few parts of my presentation to a more upbeat style, I was able to reach people in my audience that I was obviously missing before. And I am eternally grateful for that lesson!

So don't be afraid to try what you're learning from others. As my mates in the U.K. and Australasia would say, "Give it a go!" And then have the wisdom to adjust it to your own style.

Create it, then adjust it. (That, by the way, is a wonderful motto to live and work by.)

Master Prospectors Are Mentors

All the secrets you're learning about in this book came from Master Prospectors. I watched them in action. Camped out on their doorstep. Picked their brains. Moved in with them. Asked a million questions.

I made Master Prospectors my mentors.

The concept of "mentoring" is as old as the human race itself. And if it's survived all this time with flying colors, you may want to embrace it too. I did and it works.

And don't feel inhibited about asking for such a relationship with a Master Prospector. True, they already have many demands on their time. The worst thing they can say, however, is "No." And like any budding Master Prospector, you know that a "no" today is just a question of timing. Tomorrow, twelve tomorrows from now, it could be a totally different answer.

I pursued some mentors for several months before they allowed me to *really* study with them, and one in particular I "pestered" for more than a year before he brought me into his confidence. Master Prospectors know that persistence is a key to success in Network Marketing. Someone who calls consistently and isn't easily put off gets their attention.

Also, Master Prospectors have a built-in sincerity meter that tells them when a person is truthful and hard-working. The most successful people I know in this business are the ones who, despite their busy schedules, make time for the up-and-comers.

I'm not recommending that you become obnoxious or rude. I *am* recommending that you not take "no" for an answer—if you have a burning desire to learn and grow. Master Prospectors will respect and honor that quality within you.

One thing you can do to make your mentor relationship work from the start is to show your prospective Master Prospector mentor that there's something in it for him or her. Think about what you would be willing to trade for their time and teaching. If you're in their network and on a pay-out level that benefits them, consider making a commitment to a higher level of performance and ask for their partnership. If he or she is not in your upline, create another benefit that shows them that you're willing to return the favor.

The More The Merrier

And try to have more than just one Master as a mentor. The more Masters, the merrier.

Why? By having only one mentor or role model, you risk losing your own personal identity. As strongly as I encourage you to always be a great student, I recommend with equal vigor that you *never be a follower.*

Self-Mastery is not about being like someone else—it's about discovering and bringing out the best in you!

So look for the qualities in others that you would like to possess. These are your teachers—your mentors. Then isolate these qualities from the person and make them your very own.

The more qualities you want to possess, the more mentors and role models you will need, and the more diverse and balanced your life will become.

If I can leave you with something that will bring this message home, let it be this:

True Masters are teachers, not gurus with followers.

True students are future Masters, not followers of gurus.

Always be a great student, never a follower!

My Shining Light

As you may have noticed, I dedicated this book to my late father who passed away last year.

My father, John, has been a mentor of mine for many years. Not because of his entrepreneurial spirit—he chose and successfully followed the safe and sure road to financial security. He accomplished his life's goals with smart planning and by working very hard as a civil servant for more than thirty-five years. He's my mentor because he possessed a quality that I have yet to see any other man display with such mastery.

His willingness and desire to shower his wife with unconditional love, respect, passion and commitment was a sight to behold. I've never seen a man treasure a woman more than my father did my mother. The relationship they shared for fifty years was of the highest order—and will live forever!

It's sad that all the while I was growing up, surrounded by all this affection and love, I didn't truly value it. I thought, "This is the way it must be for everyone—no big deal!" It was only after I left home and experienced a couple of relationships that didn't work for me that I began to recognize how valuable a life partner can be in living a *balanced* and *abundant life*.

So now, even though you're gone, Pop, please know that you are my shining light—my example and role model of what love for your partner can truly be. Thanks to you, I'll always contribute to and expect the best between Yvonne and I.

They say that when the student is ready, the

teacher will appear. Well, Pop, it may have taken me quite a while to get ready, but thanks to your patience and everlasting example, I am *now* learning and living your lessons well!

———

The Action Step below is your opportunity to clearly focus on any mentor/student relationships you would like to create in your life. Choose your teachers carefully!

MY ACTION STEPS
to Mastery of Secret #16:
Master Prospectors study and model the Masters

1) Who are the current mentors in my life?

_____

_____

_____

_____

_____

_____

_____

_____

_____

2) **Who are the potential new mentors in my life?**

_____

_____

_____

_____

_____

_____

_____

_____

3) **What qualities do all of these mentors possess that I desire to have?**

_____

_____

_____

_____

_____

_____

_____

_____

_____

_____

4) What do I plan to do to study my mentors more
   actively and master these qualities for myself?

_____

_____

_____

_____

_____

_____

_____

_____

_____

_____

_____

_____

_____

_____

Secret #17

Master Prospectors know what they want inside their oranges!

As I've mentioned, I have many mentors in my life and one of my most valued is Dr. Wayne Dyer. To the best of my knowledge he is not building a Network Marketing business—nevertheless, he is a Master and teaches thousands of aspiring Masters valuable lessons.

On one of his audiotapes, he uses an analogy that, when I first heard it, made a lasting impact on my life. It deals with how we react when people or circumstances touch us—better yet, test us! It goes like this:

Imagine...

I would like you to imagine that I hold in my hand a fresh, ripe and juicy orange. Although I'm not an exceptionally big or strong guy, if I were to squeeze this orange, something would come out of it.

What do you think would come out of this orange when I squeezed it?

Juice, you say? Good! What kind of juice?

Orange juice? Good again! Why is it that when I squeeze this orange, orange juice comes out? Why not apple juice or pear juice or any other kind of juice?

It's an orange, John! And when you squeeze an orange, only orange juice can come out of it. Because that's what's inside of an orange—orange juice!

What's The Point, You Ask?

Good question!

Hopefully, after reading this book, you'll be so inspired that you'll pick up the phone and schedule an appointment with one of those high priority prospects you've been putting off contacting. You know, one of those prospects on your *chicken list!*

Now let's say that you prepare for this meeting like you never have before. Let's also say that you give the best presentation you've ever given. You offer your magnificent gift to this prospect with enthusiasm, professionalism, integrity, respect, and yes—love!

Now, at the end of your presentation, you mentally step back to observe their response and embrace what you believe will be their heartfelt appreciation for your time and special offering.

Instead, this prospect looks at you with distrust and disbelief and says something to you that sounds like...

"Are you crazy? You honestly thought I'd be interested in this? It's an illegal pyramid scheme, for goodness sake. I suggest you get out of this scam right now, before you lose your money. Why don't you get yourself a real job?"

Ouch!

Your prospect just squeezed you—didn't they? And let's say that out of you comes anger and self-defense; personal rejection and discouragement; maybe even doubt that what you are doing and offering to people is of value.

The question is this: *Do these feelings come out of you because of who did the squeezing? Or because of what was inside of you to begin with?*

Let's go back once again to the principle of focusing our attention and energy on what we can control and having the wisdom to release what we can't.

We can't control—or for that matter stop (unless we choose to live like a hermit)—people and circumstances from squeezing us. We are squeezed by someone or something virtually every day of our lives. We can, however, control what's inside! And if all we want in our lives is positive and abundant thinking, peace, harmony, compassion and love, then no matter who squeezes us for whatever reason, all we ever allow to come outside of us are those positive qualities. Because that's all we want to have inside of us.

Easier Said Than Done

Sounds good, doesn't it? Not so easily done, though, is it?

More than likely you'll be tested on this within a few days. Somewhere, somehow, you'll get squeezed and you'll be asked to show the world what you have inside.

Maybe you'll be driving on the freeway, late for an important meeting. Trying to make up valuable time, you're weaving in and out of traffic like world-champion race car driver, Mario Andretti.

All of a sudden, this little old lady, with blue hair and a big car, going half the speed limit, pulls out in front of you—and you can't get around her. She's making you even later than you already are—in other words, she's squeezing you.

Impulsively, you want to honk your horn, roll down your window, stick out your head and yell, "Get out of the way, you miserable old bag—I'm late for a very important meeting!"

As Dr. Dyer reminds us, "Every time we use words or actions to define someone else, all we're really doing is defining ourselves."

You see, that little old lady is exactly where she is supposed to be—she's totally on purpose. She is there to test you. She's there to see what you have inside!

To Pause Is To Think

Here's one thing that can really help us: Every time we get squeezed, *we can pause and think before we squirt.* By getting into the habit of pausing (for just a few split-seconds) every time we get squeezed, we give ourselves valuable time to think about what we want inside—before we display it.

Impulsive behavior often doesn't afford us the luxury of thought and choice! Unless, of course, we have conditioned our impulsive behavior to always reflect what we want inside.

So the next time some uneducated, negative prospect squeezes you, *pause*—so you can think and choose. Since life is all about making choices, you can either:

1) Squirt them with doubt, anger, and discouragement, and leave them with an indelible stain. Or:

2) Spray them with a gentle, cooling mist of compassion, understanding, and respect.

The choice is yours. What you have inside is yours, too. And everyday it's there for the world to see—and for you to live with.

So let's now take a look at *how*—what we have inside—is formed and created. And, if we choose, how we can change it!

It's All B. S.

Each of us has a set of beliefs about who we are and what we can or cannot accomplish in life. It's called our Belief System. I call it B.S.—not because it isn't powerful or real, *but because most of us are victims of our belief system and not Masters of it.*

Do you know what a belief really is?

It's a habit we have—a habit of thought. And like many of our other habits of thought, it was given to us freely—and for free. Remember Secret #15: **Master Prospectors know something for nothing is usually good for nothing?**

Let me explain.

The beliefs we have about what we can or cannot accomplish in life began to be formed way back when you and I were kids. We learned early on that there were limits to what we could do, have and be.

There were places we could go and not go; things we could do and not do; words we could say and not say; thoughts we could think and not think.

Now I'm not making a good or bad judgement here. This is just the way life is and it's pretty much the same for everybody—Master Prospectors included.

What's important to realize is that our beliefs started as something for nothing. We didn't ask for them or pay for them, and we actually did very little to consciously select or choose them. We just got the input—mostly from authority figures like parents, relatives, teachers, and the like—and when we got it frequently (or loudly) enough, we took it to heart and soon it became a *habit of thought*.

You see, a habit is something we do *without thinking*. It's programmed in. All we do is react the way we're programmed. So when we're squeezed by one of life's encounters that doesn't go the way we want, our true beliefs about ourselves are revealed.

Now none of this programming was necessarily the *truth*. Good, bad, or indifferent, it was just what it was and is just what it is today. We were programmed with beliefs about ourselves and our world based on the beliefs of others—based on what *they* thought or felt was true.

And, unfortunately, most of this programming was about what we *shouldn't* or *couldn't* do, have, or be.

No... No... NO!

"Don't touch—that's HOT!... Don't play in the street... Don't play with matches...."

Hey, it kept us safe. It was for our own good—right?

Do you know that the average kid hears the word "no" seventeen times more often in a day than the word "yes?" It's true. For every fourteen positives that are communicated in a normal childhood day, there are 240 negatives.

Something for nothing in a very big way.

Can you see how most of us began to receive a pretty big chunk of negative programming at an early age—and how that programming has been kept up-to-date for quite some time now?

Why is it so important for us to know this?

It's proven we can only accomplish what we *believe* we can accomplish. You know that famous quote—"Whatever the mind of man can conceive and believe, it can achieve"? Well, here's perhaps the most important secret of all the secrets of the Master Prospectors:

Master Prospectors believe that they are Master Prospectors.

If they didn't believe it, they couldn't be it.

Squeeze a Master Prospector and watch what comes out!

They listen, they think, and they smile. Then they begin to ask questions to help the other person reveal their doubts and fears. Master Prospectors focus on getting rid of the emotional charge or upset they may be experiencing before they squirt. The Master Prospector is secure in his or her success. The Master Prospector isn't filled with doubts and fears. And if by chance (because Master Prospectors are human) doubt, fear, and personal discouragement do cross their mind—they recognize them for what they are—*untruths*. So they focus their attention on releasing them by reversing them.

That's their most profound secret.

What Do You Believe?

Do you believe you can be a Master Prospector?

I'll tell you this right now: If you don't believe you can be a Master Prospector, there is absolutely no way in heaven—or on earth—that you will ever become one. And that, my friends, is the truth!

Okay, so what if, right now, you don't see yourself as a Master Prospector? What if that's just not a realistic possibility for you? Is it time to give up your dream of a successful business and call it quits?

I understand how some of you may have those thoughts. It's okay.

But please, don't call it quits. I've got great news—it's the secret to all the secrets. It's about what I said in the beginning of this secret—about how our beliefs are just our habits.

How To Change Your Beliefs
(Your Habits)

This exercise is called, "Knowing What You Want In-side *Your* Orange." I could also call this, "How to Cre-ate *Something for Something.*" Here's how it goes:

First of all, based on what you've learned so far about the secrets of the Master Prospectors, write out in the space below a detailed description of what you believe a Master Prospector looks, sounds, and feels like. Now don't worry, this isn't about you—this is about defining the *ideal* Master Prospector.

Make this person the same age and sex as you are now, but as you write the rest of the picture, forget about you. In as much rich detail as possible, describe this image of the perfect Master Prospector. Write about all the things he or she would do and the kind of attitude and approach he or she would use. Please do this now.

In fact, if you choose to pass over this exercise, you may want to ask yourself, "Why am I reading this book?" That's how important this exercise is—if you truly want to become a Master Prospector.

Here's an idea that can help you: Review the Ac-tion Steps you completed in the previous secrets. The ideal Master Prospector is made up of many of the qualities contained in them.

_____

_____

_____

_____

_____

_____

_____

_____

_____

_____

_____

_____

_____

_____

_____

_____

_____

_____

_____

Okay, now I want you to go back over your picture of this perfect Master Prospector and fill in *even more details*. Make this picture even more vivid and alive.

And one more thing: This time, add *your name and face* throughout your description.

I don't care whether or not you *believe* this picture. Just put yourself in there as the Master Prospector you are describing.

Go ahead, fill in the picture of you as a Master
Prospector. Do it now.

Me, the Master Prospector

_____

_____

_____

_____

_____

_____

_____

_____

_____

_____

_____

_____

_____

_____

_____

_____

_____

_____

Great! I want to thank you for completing this exercise. In fact, why don't you go ahead and thank yourself, too. You did all the work, and, believe me, you'll enjoy the rewards!

Now if this is the very first time you've done anything like this, you might be feeling a little silly. You might be thinking: "That's not *me*." And if it is, it's a lie—right?

I understand those thoughts—those habits. Usually everybody has them when they first create a picture like this. But here's what I want you to realize: *You also created the idea that this isn't you!*

Either picture, *you created it.*

It has nothing to do with whether or not these pictures are true. Both pictures are made-up: you as not-a-Master-Prospector, with all your doubts, fears, and limitations; and you as-a-Master-Prospector, with the description you just wrote. You created both of them in your mind. And since you are the creator, you have the right to choose what to keep and what to throw away. So why not keep the one that empowers you and throw away the one that doesn't?

Is it empowering to hold in your mind a picture of you as limited, incapable, and not-a-Master-Prospector?

No! Then throw it away and replace it with your new, empowering picture. Look at your new picture as a tool for you to use, to be as successful as you choose. It's a creative tool, just like a video or a business card, only this time you're going to *give it to you,* instead of to your prospects.

And here's how you do that.

The Habit Of Being A Master Prospector

I'm going to show you how to get into the habit of being a Master Prospector.

Here's the key: You create this habit like every other habit you have, by doing it again and again, over and over, *until you literally become a Master Prospector.*

To begin, type up the description that you just wrote down of yourself as a Master Prospector so it fits on one page. Then put a copy in a clear plastic sleeve in your daily planner. Have two or three other copies around as well.

Read this description twenty (that's right—twenty!) times each and every day from now on.

Read it first thing when you wake up and make it the last thing you do before you go to bed. Also read it every half hour or so throughout the day.

Now the reason for this is simple: The mind is *quantitative, not qualitative.* That is, it doesn't recognize the difference between the input you give it from the page you just wrote or the thoughts you already have. Your mind doesn't distinguish which one of these are real or, for that matter, true! It just takes them all in and lets them stack up. If the stack that says you aren't a Master Prospector is bigger than the one that says you are, the mind concludes that you're not and that's that.

All we're doing here is balancing the scales—only this time, *in your favor!*

Do you get the idea? Can you see what we're up to here?

There's no hocus-pocus to this. We're just setting it up so that you're replacing a disempowering habit of thought with an empowering one. (By the way, you can use this same technique with anything you want to achieve.)

Now, after you've done your daily reading for a while, and you decide you want to turbo-charge this process, take your written description and read it into a cassette player. Then play your tape back while you read along with your written Master Prospector description.

If you think reading it over and over is powerful, just imagine what happens when you read it and hear it at the same time!

Try It—You Might Like It

It won't affect my belief system if you believe this technique will work or not. All I ask is that you try it for one month and see what happens. When you do, I'd wager a fortune that you will be both pleased and amazed at the changes you'll experience in your thinking and your actions.

Remember, thoughts take root in the mind and grow into actions in the world. Just imagine what would happen if you had the habit of thought that *you are a Master Prospector,* and if you held that belief foremost in your mind!

That's the kind of belief system that leads to what Master Prospectors call *massive action!* And all it takes for you to experience that yourself is an investment of your time, effort, and energy to reprogram your habits of belief. So take the exercise I've just suggested and do it!

I challenge you to squeeze *that* for a while and then watch the MASTER in you come out!

———————

At the risk of sounding like I'm trying to squeeze you, guess what time it is? That's right, it's Action Step time! So get to it, because you're going to *love* what comes out of you as a result of this secret!

MY ACTION STEPS
to Mastery of Secret #17:

Master Prospectors know what they want inside their oranges!

1) When someone or something squeezes me, what do I want to come outside? What am I committed to *being*?

———————————————————————

———————————————————————

———————————————————————

———————————————————————

———————————————————————

———————————————————————

———————————————————————

———————————————————————

———————————————————————

———————————————————————

2) When I do get squeezed, what two things must I discipline myself to do before I impulsively squirt?

    1. _____

    2. _____

3) I agree to complete the exercise outlined in this secret entitled, "Me, the Master Prospector." My dated signature is my personal commitment to complete and implement this exercise.

    Signature: _____

    Dated: _____

Master Prospectors love to play the game

*W*ell, my friend, you've come this far. That tells me you're a serious student.

The path of Mastery beckons you, and I sense you are moving towards it with an open heart and a beginner's mind—two of the most treasured qualities of the Masters themselves.

So I'm seizing this one last opportunity to "add value" to your journey, and it's with this Bonus Secret. Consider it my gift to you: a well-deserved acknowledgment of your commitment to be the best that you can be!

The Game Of Life

One of Shakespeare's characters said that all the world is a stage and that we're merely players. Well, here's a slightly different twist on that old bit of wisdom.

Randy Ward, a very dear friend of mine, wrote the exceptional book *Winning the Greatest Game of All—Network Marketing*. In it, Randy helps us look at our business as an *accelerated game of life!* And, as with all games, we have a choice: we can play or we can watch!

You see, the game of Network Marketing is like any other game: there are spectators, players, rules, winners, losers, run-of-the-mill performers and superstars. Given that, what role do *you choose* to play?

In the game of Network Marketing, Master Prospectors are the superstars. They're the ones the people pay to see. They're the ones the team counts on to pull them through. They're team captains, and they always bring out the best in their teammates.

If you follow any professional sport like tennis, baseball, basketball, football, soccer, cricket or golf, you've probably noticed that the greatest of the greats all have one thing in common—they love the game. The monster salaries they earn is one of the by-products of that love. That's the secret within Secret #1: **Master Prospectors don't sit on their assets.**

Paid What We're Worth

And while I'm on this subject of monster salaries, it amazes me how some people complain about what they call "outrageous incomes" that the Masters of professional sports earn. One reason Master athletes earn "outrageous incomes" is because *they believe they're worth it!*

Obviously, someone else does, too—the person who pays him. In fact, every time I go to a game with my wife and friends, *I'm buying into what those Master athletes believe they're worth.* And I'll continue to buy into their belief until the value I receive from watching them is not as great as the value of the dollars I pay for a ticket! More than likely, so will you—so will everyone!

My point is this: If some day you'd like to earn an "outrageous income" like the Master Prospectors of Network Marketing, then keep doing everything you can to build your image of self-worth.

Why? Because the marketplace, my friend, will pay you anything you *truly believe* you're worth. And it will continue to pay you that for as long as you deliver equal or greater value in return—no matter how "outrageous" your income may appear to others!

We don't live in a world that limits the number of people who can earn outrageous incomes. *There is no scarcity of abundance. There is only a scarcity of abundant thinking and teaching.*

So build *abundance* in your mind and *value* in your work. Then have the guts to ask the marketplace to pay you for that value. How else are you ever going to know what you're capable of earning? More importantly, how else are you ever going to know *what value you're capable of producing?*

Practice, Practice, Practice

Another thing about the greats in any game is that they have a fantastic work ethic.

Some of us are born with a special gift or talent,

and perhaps you're one of them. If so, I'm sure you count your blessings every night before you go to sleep. The fact is that far more men and women were born with just average talents and then had to work hard at becoming great. That's the road most of us have to take.

Larry Bird was one of basketball's greatest players, and he got that way because he practiced more diligently than anyone else. Hours before each game, Larry was on the court shooting foul shots. Between seasons he played and practiced for hours every day. He was an average athlete who worked very hard, and all that hard work—not raw talent—will earn him an honored spot in basketball's Hall of Fame.

Master Prospectors work hard, too—even those who seem to be born to it. If you want to know the secret of making big money in Network Marketing, just look at Master Prospectors. While other people talk to two or three people a day and earn monthly checks of $500, $1,000 or $2,000, Master Prospectors talk to twenty or thirty people a day and earn $20,000, $30,000 or $100,000 per month and more. That's the difference: practice, practice, practice. And that's the secret within Secret #2: **Master Prospectors are consistently consistent.**

The Heavy-Hitter Syndrome

Master Prospectors don't count on making just the "big plays," either—although they often do.

Lots of people assume that the key to success in Network Marketing is to sponsor a "heavy-hitter"— someone with a huge circle of influence and a lot of experience. That's not necessarily the case. Most so-

called heavy-hitters had to emerge from the rank-
and-file players. Remember the "Magical Genie" in
Secret #5 who showed you that the great leaders of
your network three years from now are people you
haven't met yet? More importantly, they're people
who don't even know that they're heavy-hitters yet!
So sponsor and treat everyone as if they already
were.

Stick To The Basics

Day-in and day-out, Master Prospectors do the basics. They know that those solid, simple efforts done
with consistency are the ones that pay off the biggest
and the best in the long run.

Sure, we're all impressed when we see that towering, game-winning home run, or a long, tricky putt
that drops in the cup to win a golf tournament. But
the truth is that small successes—*consistently delivered*—win championships.

Let me tell you a story to illustrate the power of
small successes.

The Ring Toss Game

I recently attended a fantastic workshop. It was a 3½-
day-long affair with all kinds of wonderful people
from a variety of fields. It was geared around experi-
ential training and much of it was based on playing
games. At the end of each game, we'd review it and
see what insights we could discover about ourselves
through our behavior.

It's a very elementary, yet powerful principle: We
play our games like we play our life. Many carnival
and children's games are similar in purpose and out-

come to the games we play in our personal and professional lives.

So, by standing back and observing our behavior—
especially with the insight and input from some
knowledgeable instructors—we can learn some valuable lessons.

This one game was really fascinating. It was called
the Ring Toss. Everyone in the class had an opportunity to buy these rings for a dollar each. It wasn't
mandatory to play, and, of course, a few chose not to.

At one end of the room the organizers lined up a
number of stakes on the floor. Back from the stakes
were markers—strips of tape on the carpet that your
toes had to stay behind while you tossed rings onto
the stakes.

The first marker was about six feet away from the
stake. If you got a ring on the stake from that distance, you got two dollars, or double your money.

There were markers all the way back to about
thirty feet behind the stake, and the money you received for getting the ring on the stake from those
greater distances went up and up, the farther back
you stood. If you tossed a ring around a stake from
ten feet away you'd earn twenty dollars and from
thirty feet you'd earn a cool one hundred bucks. Not
bad for a one dollar investment—right?

Now most people bought four or five rings and
stood somewhere between the six and ten foot markers and started tossing. A couple of people went all
the way to the very last marker and started sailing
rings from back there.

Guess what—nobody made a "ringer." Not one ring over a stake.

We all looked at each other. Some of the people decided the game was either too hard or "rigged" and they quit. Others—myself included—decided to hang around to see if we could figure out how to win the game.

Finally, one woman bought five rings. She walked up to that very first marker set back about six feet behind the stake, leaned out as far as she could and tossed the rings one at a time at the stake. She got only one ringer out of the five attempts. She lost money—three dollars, to be exact!

She then went back and bought another five rings for a dollar each. I remember saying to myself, "She's sure a glutton for punishment. She can't win with those odds."

She stood again at the six-foot marker and leaned over as far as she could, nearly falling forward and crossing the line, and tossed another four rings. No ringers and another four bucks lost! She stood there looking frustrated but optimistic, because she believed there was a way of winning this game.

After thinking for a moment, she took her last ring, positioned her toes carefully behind the marker and leaned forward once again. This time she let herself gently fall parallel to the ground towards the stake. Her toes however, were still behind the marker. She then stretched out and dropped the ring over the stake—*ringer!*

She quickly looked up at the instructor—no whistle, no horn, no foul! Her toes were still behind the marker!

Immediately, she ran over to the person selling the rings, pulled out her American Express Gold Card and told him, "I want to purchase one ring for a dollar, and every time I use it, charge me another dollar for it."

She ran back to the six foot marker and did the same thing as before, except this time she didn't drop the ring over the stake. She continued to hold onto it and placed the ring on and off the stake as fast as the instructor could count. After thirty-five successful ringers—in well under a minute—the instructor blew the whistle and announced that she was the winner of the game.

If It Works

Thanks to this creative, courageous and lateral-thinking lady, what lessons do you think we all learned? There were two:

1) Even though rules are *not* meant to be broken, they *are* meant to be challenged. So it's okay to question and stretch the *perceived* rules of a game, as long as you put no one at risk other than yourself. (Unless, of course, the others at risk clearly understand the risk beforehand and agree!)

2) When you discover something that works and you know you can do it, do it as often and as fast as you can. (Make it a part of your daily routine!)

Try looking at it this way. After you read this book, I am confident you're going to move towards something that you've learned and give it your best effort.

When it works for you—and you know you can

guarantee a predictable, positive result every time you do it, then do it as often and as fast as you can— even if the result only *appears* to be an infield hit in a game applauded for its towering home runs.

Why? Because you know you can do it every time. And, over time, those small successes will add up to win you the BIG game!

Then when that irresistible urge comes over you— and you know the urge I'm talking about, the one that tells you "Swing for the fences, go for the big home run"—you can "go for it" if it feels right.

How do you know when it feels right? When you know that winning the game doesn't depend on hitting that home run!

Master The Game

Master Prospectors don't spend all their time seeking that one-in-a-million superstar. They don't run one big expensive ad and hope someone who calls will earn them a million. They take those simple, solid steps they've mastered and do them over and over again. They do the basics every day and they're rewarded by the awesome power of duplication.

The Master Prospecting game is the greatest game of all in Network Marketing. Once you know the secrets—and by now you've been exposed to eighteen—it's simply a question of practice until you master them.

The Master Game in any endeavor is not for everyone. Master Prospecting is a demanding game, because it requires you to be the best that you can be— and that's a lot. It takes work and some sacrifice, and it's possible that others will not understand the path you're on and choose to criticize you.

The truth is, most of the people in the world aren't up to the Master Game. Are you? Do you believe that the Master Prospector game is one worth playing?

If your answer is yes, please read this quote. You may wish to read it three or four times over. It's from Robert S. DeRopp and it's called *The Master Game:*

> Seek, above all, for a game worth playing. Such is the advice of the oracle to modern man. Having found the game play it with intensity—play as if your life and sanity depended on it. (They do depend on it.) Follow the example of the French Existentialists and flourish a banner bearing the word "Engagement." Though nothing means anything and all roads are marked "No Exit," yet move as if your movements had some purpose. If life does not seem to offer a game worth playing, then invent one. For it must be clear, even to the most clouded intelligence, that any game is better than no game.

> But although it is safe to play The Master Game, this has not served to make it popular. It still remains the most demanding and difficult of games and in our society, there are few who play. Contemporary man, hypnotized by the glitter of his own gadgets, has little contact with his inner world, a vast and complex territory about which men know very little. The aim of the game is true awakening, full development of the powers latent in man. The game can be played only by people whose observations of themselves and others have led them to a certain conclusion, namely, that man's ordinary state of consciousness, his so-

called waking state, is not the highest level of consciousness of which he is capable. In fact, this state is so far from real awakening that it could appropriately be called a form of somnambulism, a condition of "waking sleep."

Once a person has reached this conclusion, he is no longer able to sleep comfortably. A new appetite develops within him, the hunger for real awakening, for full consciousness. He realizes that he sees, hears, and knows only a tiny fraction of what he could see, hear and know; that he lives in the poorest, shabbiest of the rooms in his inner dwelling, and that he could enter other rooms, beautiful and filled with treasures, the windows of which look out on eternity and infinity.

The solitary player lives today in a culture that is more or less totally opposed to the aims he has set for himself; that does not recognize the existence of The Master Game, and regards players of this game as slightly queer or mad. The player thus confronts great opposition from the culture in which he lives and must strive with forces which tend to bring his game to a halt before it has even started. Only by finding a teacher and becoming part of the group of pupils that that teacher has collected around him can the player find encouragement and support. Otherwise he simply forgets his aim, or wanders off down some side road and loses himself.

Here it is sufficient to say that The Master Game can NEVER be made easy to play. It demands all that a man has; all his feelings, all his thought, his entire resources, physical and spiritual. If he tries to play it in a halfhearted way or tries to get results by unlawful means, he runs the risk of destroying his own potential. For this reason it is better not to embark on the game at all than to [do] it halfheartedly.

Like I said, if you really want to *own* the powerful message here, read this quote three or four times. When you've done that, I have some final words I'd like to share with you.

Please invest a little extra time with this Action Step—it's the springboard to your future in Network Marketing!

MY ACTION STEPS

to Mastery of The Bonus Secret:

Master Prospectors love to play the game

1) Which secrets am I most attracted to and want to act on first and foremost? (Number them in their order of importance. You can use the Table of Contents as a reference guide.)

Secret #	Rank	Secret #	Rank
One	_____	Six	_____
Two	_____	Seven	_____
Three	_____	Eight	_____
Four	_____	Nine	_____
Five	_____	Ten	_____

Secret #	Rank	Secret #	Rank
Eleven	_____	Fifteen	_____
Twelve	_____	Sixteen	_____
Thirteen	_____	Seventeen	_____
Fourteen	_____	Bonus	_____

2) What business-building activities *that I do now* generate positive and predictable results when I do them?

_____

_____

_____

_____

_____

_____

_____

_____

_____

_____

_____

_____

_____

_____

_____

3) Which of the previous activities can I do bigger, better and faster to accelerate my results? And how will I accomplish that?

_____

_____

_____

_____

_____

_____

_____

_____

_____

_____

_____

_____

_____

Epilogue

*I*n the very beginning of this book, I told you that my job was to help you become competent at prospecting. I also wrote that with that competence, you would develop the confidence you needed to feel truly comfortable with prospecting. And once you were comfortable, you'd be well on your way to being a Master Prospector.

I keep thinking about that last part: "You'd be well on your way to being a Master Prospector."

The truth is, you were well on your way the moment you picked up this book.

You see, *Mastery is not a destination.* You don't show up all of a sudden—*poof!*—as a card-carrying Master Prospector. It's not some place to get to. It's not the end result of achievement like a black belt or a graduate degree. You don't *do* Mastery. Mastery is a state of *being. Mastery is a journey*, and, my friend, you are clearly on the path *right now*. For that, I want to congratulate you and acknowledge you.

Mastery Defined

I would like you to read something I've kept from a 1987 issue of *Esquire* magazine devoted to Mastery. It beautifully describes what I'm talking about.

> It resists definition, yet can be instantly recognized. It comes in many variations, yet follows certain unchanging laws. It makes us, in the words of the Olympic motto, "faster, higher, stronger," yet is not really a goal or destination, but rather a process, or journey.

> We call this journey *Mastery* and tend to assume that it requires a special ticket available only to those born with exceptional abilities. But Mastery is not reserved for the super-talented, or even for those who are fortunate enough to have gotten an early start. It is available to anyone who is willing to get on the path and stay on it—regardless of age, sex, or experience.

> The problem is that we have few, if any, maps to guide us on the journey, or even to show us how to find the path. The modern world can be viewed as a prodigious conspiracy against Mastery. We are bombarded with promises of fast, immediate gratification and instant success, all of which lead in exactly the wrong direction.

> (Playing For Keeps: The Art of Mastery in Sports and Life, *Esquire*, May 1987, edited by George Leonard.)

I wrote this book to help you *find* and *stay* on your path of Mastery in Network Marketing. I also intended this book to be your trustworthy friend—a map to help guide you along your chosen path.

As the *Esquire* article cautioned, there are no "shortcuts." Although you may be fortunate enough to experience quick results and some "instant success" (and yes, there's enough great information here to provide you with a ton of powerful tools and techniques to do that), it's more important that you "get" the essence of Mastery.

Also keep in mind that everyone's path is different. Yours is unique: it will not look like anybody else's. The speed with which you travel your path will not be the same, either. You will go a bit slower than some, much faster than others. The key is getting on the path—your own special path—and staying on it.

You've Got What It Takes!

Mastery requires one more thing!

The reason most people don't achieve Mastery is because they don't have this. They lack this one characteristic that I believe you possess.

Do you know what it is? Think about it for a moment. What could you possibly have that others lack?

It's called *courage*!

It may be hard for you to believe, but it's true. The only reason you are on your path of Mastery and countless others are still dreaming and hoping about it is because you have courage and they don't.

You see, courage is made up of three words. And when you truly understand what these three words are, you'll know exactly why you have courage and why so many of your people that you try to motivate don't. More importantly, you'll know how to instill courage in your people and help them start (and continue) on their own path of Mastery.

Here are the three words that define courage.

The **first** is *commitment*. A commitment to being the best that you can be. Obviously you have that because you've started and completed this book.

The **third** is *action*—a willingness to act upon your commitment. The Action Steps to Mastery that you defined at the end of each secret will now become your plan of action—your personal path to becoming a Master Prospector. And I am confident that *you will act* on your plan.

It's the second word—the one *between* commitment and action—that truly defines courage.

In fact, if this word didn't exist, you wouldn't know what courage was! No, it's not *fear*—but you're close!

The **second** word is *doubt!*

You see, the difference between you and all those you have unsuccessfully tried to motivate to pursue their vision is that you've learned how to have your doubts—but *do it anyway!* You've learned how to process doubt and work through it. Most of your people are still stuck in doubt. So instead of having their doubts—*their doubts have them.*

Sure, you have doubts. We all do. Doubt is the very next thing that we experience when we commit to something. Doubt is part of the package, part of the deal. You can't have commitment without doubt.

The reason you have courage is because you rise above your doubts into the bright light of action.

So, courage, my friend, is not the absence of doubt—it is Mastery over doubt!

That's Why You're On Your Way

Remember when I said to you earlier that you were well on your way to becoming a Master Prospector the moment you picked up this book?

Do you know how I knew that? Because you've completed this book. Think back on all the doubts you've had to deal with along the way. Yet you still took the actions necessary to complete the journey and finish this book.

Why? You know why! Because *you're committed to being the best that you can be*—that's why! And when doubt entered your mind, you simply reminded yourself of your vision and your commitment to it— that clear and bright vision of who you want to be. And it's both the memory and the brightness of your vision that gave you the courage to master doubt.

That, by the way, is how you help instill courage in your people. Constantly remind them of what *they want to be*. Help them create their own vision and keep it in front of them as much as possible.

Then, when they start to give you excuses for not acting on what needs to be done, tell them exactly where they are—stuck in doubt. And while looking them straight in the eye, also tell them that the only thing that is stopping them from *being* their vision is their lack of courage to act on it.

So, Master Prospector, I want to acknowledge you one more time for your vision and your courage to act on it. And I want to encourage you to stay forever on your path of Mastery.

I mean, look at how far you've already come. And, as we both know, you truly deserve *to be the best that you can be.*

Have a glorious and abundant journey.

Your friend and fellow traveler,

John

ABOUT THE AUTHOR

"When I founded Millionaires in Motion in 1985," says John Kalench, "the Network Marketing industry had a very real need for a no-nonsense approach to education. Millionaires in Motion has come a long way in filling that gap."

A leading trainer, consultant and visionary for the Network Marketing industry, John Kalench was first introduced to Network Marketing in 1979. Over the next eight years, John built three highly profitable distributorships and was also the President, CEO and controlling stockholder in his own Network Marketing company.

In 1985, John was positioned atop a network of thousands of distributors nationwide. He created Millionaires in Motion (MIM) to provide specialized training programs for his network.

John's training programs were immediately embraced by his sales leaders throughout the country, and, in February of 1987, he decided to make MIM an independent training company for the entire Network Marketing industry. To meet this objective, MIM divorced itself from financial interest in any particular company—training and consulting would be its only business.

Since then, thousands of Network Marketing entrepreneurs have attended John's seminars and graduated from his workshops all over the world. Top sales leaders and company principals have also used his consulting expertise to better direct and expand their business strategies.

For two consecutive years, MIM received the President's award for training excellence from the MLMIA (Multi-Level Marketing International Association).

"Our mission is clear," says John. "We want you to think of us as your Global Ambassadors of Network Marketing."

MIM International Agents

Would you like Network Marketing to work for you in a bigger and more profitable way? Then contact the MIM agent in your part of the world for a *free* catalog of MIM's educational materials, a volume discount schedule and MIM's international schedule of training workshops and seminars.

NORTH AMERICAN CORPORATE OFFICE

Millionaires in Motion (MIM)
6821 Convoy Court
San Diego, CA 92111 USA
Tel (619) 467 9667
Fax (619) 467 9504
Toll-free order line:
800 388 1748

SOUTH PACIFIC HEADQUARTERS

Spectrum Marketing Services
P.O. Box 264
Toorak
Victoria 3142
Australia
Tel 61 3 824 7938
Fax 61 3 824 7200
Toll-free order line:
1 800 808 255

EUROPEAN HEADQUARTERS

MLM International
5 Cornwall Crescent
London W11 1PH
United Kingdom
Tel 44 71 221 5611
Fax 44 71 221 5610

ITALY

Multi-Level Marketing
 International
Corso Matteotti 38
I-25122 Brescia
Tel 39 30 375 58 59
Fax 39 30 375 57 17

GERMANY

Multi-Level Marketing
 International GmbH
Braunegger Str. 64-66
D-78462 Konstanz
Tel 49 7531 90 66 66
or 49 7531 90 66 67
Fax 49 7531 90 66 70

SWITZERLAND

Multi-Level Marketing
 International Est.
Postfach 1147
Herrengasse 23
FL-9490 Vaduz
Liechtenstein
Tel 41 7523 245 21
Fax 41 7523 254 56

AUSTRIA

Multi-Level Marketing
 International
Magerbach 1A
A-6425 Haiming
Tel 43 5266 886 99
Fax 43 5266 874 72

HOLLAND/BELGIUM

Multi-Level Marketing
 International B.V.
Weerdskampweg 21A
5222 BA 's-Hertogenbosch
The Netherlands
Tel 31 73 210430
Fax 31 73 210068

FRANCE

Contact MLM International
European Headquarters
London

Would You Like Our Help?

No matter where you are in the world, MIM has tools designed to help you build and support a highly successful Network Marketing business. We offer the best educational materials available in the industry, and all of them carry the MIM 100% satisfaction guarantee.

Handsome **quantity discount pricing** is available on all materials by John Kalench and most other authors.

Call us TODAY

For Your FREE Resource Catalog and Discount Schedule

In North America

Millionaires in Motion (MIM)
6821 Convoy Court
San Diego, CA USA 92111
Call Toll Free: 800-388-1748
or Call: 619-467-9667
or Fax: 619-467-9504

Outside of North America

Refer to the preceding page for the MIM International Agent in your part of the world. Your agent will be happy to take your order, answer questions and send you a FREE resource catalog.

Best Selling Books
by John Kalench

Being the Best You Can Be in MLM. *Considered by many to be the "bible" of the Network Marketing industry, John's friendly, step-by-step approach teaches you how to build the business of your dreams. $14.95*^{U.S.}
Currently available in English, Finnish, French, & German; in Italian & Spanish by the end of 1994.

The Greatest Opportunity In The History of The World. *A great prospecting tool, this fast-reading book establishes the truths and dispels the myths about the past, present and future of the Network Marketing industry. $9.95*^{U.S.}
Currently available in English, German & Italian; in French & Spanish by the end of 1994.

17 Secrets of the Master Prospectors. *The most powerful principles and techniques used by the best in Network Marketing-all over the world—contains Action Steps for mastery of each secret. $14.95*^{U.S.}

Best Selling Books
by Other Authors

WAVE 3: The New Era In Network Marketing. *In Richard Poe's new book, you'll see how network marketers are changing the way we live and work by using a 21st century network of systems, procedures and technology that simplifies, standardizes and automates even the most difficult aspects of a Network Marketing business. $14.95*^{U.S.}

The Greatest Networker In The World. *The narrator of this fable by John Milton Fogg spends an enlightening week with the Greatest Networker, absorbing lessons about purpose, beliefs, leadership and more.* **$9.95**^{U.S.}

Street Smart Networking. *Build a powerfully successful Network Marketing business by using Robert Butwin's "street smart" tips for avoiding the pitfalls, sand traps and dark back alleys of learning the hard way.* **$9.95** *U.S.*

Instant Rapport. *Michael Brooks leads you through powerful NLP (Neuro-Linguistic Programming) techniques for rapport-building in this easy-to-read book.* **$14.95** *U.S.*

The "Big Al" Series. *Tom Schreiter shares his humorous and effective ideas on MLM leadership, recruiting, sorting and prospecting in his five book series. Ask about the "Big Al" series special.* **$12.95** *U.S each.*

Winning the Greatest Game of All—Network Marketing. *Randy Ward teaches you the subtle differences between earning $20,000 and $200,000 a year in Network Marketing—from a "big picture" perspective.* **$9.95** *U.S.*

Streamlined Bookkeeping for MLM. *Audrey Scannell offers simple methods for keeping accurate records for your accountant as well as complete instructions for preparing your own income statement.* **$7.95** *U.S.*

Audio/Video Home Study Programs by John Kalench

Being the Best You Can Be in MLM *(6 Audios). If you liked the book, you'll love listening to this six tape series while in your car and other places where you just can't read.* **$39.95** *U.S.*

"The Start of Something Big" Home Study Action Course *(7 Audios/2 Workbooks). The Action Course will focus your thoughts and activities into a specific six-week plan of action to accomplish what would ordinarily take six months to a year.* **$149.95** *U.S.*

Mind Waves For Success *(4 Audios). Each hour-long audio tape contains a subliminal message designed to raise your level of success in Goal Getting, Personal Prosperity, Health & Harmony or Service & Contribution. All you consciously hear is soothing, non-hypnotic ocean waves. Subconsciously, you're programming your mind for success.* **$49.95** *U.S.*

The Trilogy Series

Nothing beats a live presentation by John Kalench, so MIM has created this series of video/audio programs featuring John—live! Now you can bring John into your living room, to training meetings and to your prospects. Ask us about our special "buy two, get one free" offer.

Your Fast Track To Network Marketing Success
(2 Audios/Video). You only have one chance to give your business a fast start. Master the fast-start principles taught in John's live seminar by using these audio & video cassettes. **$34.95** *U.S.*

If You Knew What I Know... A Two-Hour Live Interview With John Kalench
(2 Audios/Video). This series is full of training tips and insights great for new prospects as well as for use as a training tool for your current business builders. **$34.95** *U.S.*

Build Your Vision...
(Audio/Video). John Kalench uses his heart-to-heart style to discuss the importance of vision in creating your successful Network Marketing business and the four cornerstones upon which that vision must be built. **$34.95** *U.S.*

Generic Prospecting Tools

The Greatest Opportunity In the History of the World Family of Prospecting Tools *(Book, Brochure, Audio, Video).This series of generic prospecting tools by Millionaires in Motion allows you to hand your prospects the perfect response to their questions about the Network Marketing industry—in whichever format best suits their personal style.*

Ask about mix & match quantity discounts and save up to 75% on these tools.

The Book. *100 easy-to-read pages dispel the myths and establish the truth about Network Marketing.* **$9.95** *U.S.*
Available in English, German & Italian; in French & Spanish by the end of 1994.

The Brochure. *This inexpensive "give-away" will pique your prospect's interest in the Network Marketing industry, explain the other "Greatest Opportunity..." educational materials available to them and then direct them to you for more information.* **5.00^{U.S.}$ for a package of 50**

The Video. *An emotionally compelling 20-minute video about the Network Marketing industry is hosted by John Kalench.* **15.95^{U.S.}$**

The Audio. *In this 30 minute audio based on the book, your prospect will discover the limitless opportunity of Network Marketing.* **5.95^{U.S.}$**

Turning Dreams Into Reality *(Video). This highly informative video explains the generic concepts of Network Marketing and outlines the duplication process.* **15.95^{U.S.}$**

Shelter From The Storm *(Video). What shelter do you have from the economic storm that rains harder each day? This 6-minute video paints a dramatic picture of the exceptional alternative to convention business that Network Marketing offers in today's economy.* **12.95^{U.S.}$**

Advertisement Free Industry Publications

Upline™ Magazine. *This is the industry's best monthly training publication. For subscription information, contact Upline™, 310 East Main St., Suite 150, Charlottesville, VA 22902. Tel. (804) 979 4427. Fax (804) 979 1602.*

Down-Line News. *Down-Line News is a bi-monthly newsletter providing objective information about the Network Marketing industry. For subscription information, contact Down-Line News, 330 East 63rd Street, Suite 7K, New York, NY 10021. Tel. (212) 355-1071. Fax (212) 888-8172.*